CRYSTAL FLOWERS

FLORINE STETTHEIMER, 1917-1920

FLORINE STETTHEIMER

CRYSTAL FLOWERS
POEMS AND A LIBRETTO

EDITED BY IRENE GAMMEL AND SUZANNE ZELAZO

BookThug | Toronto

MMX

FIRST BOOKTHUG EDITION

SECOND PRINTING

Introduction and notes © Irene Gammel & Suzanne Zelazo, 2010

LIBRARY AND ARCHIVES CANADA
CATALOGUING IN PUBLICATION

Stettheimer, Florine, 1871-1944
          Crystal flowers : poems and a libretto / Florine
Stettheimer ; edited
by Irene Gammel and Suzanne Zelazo.

(Department of reissue ; no. 5)
Originally publ.: New York : Privately printed, 1949.
ISBN 978-1-897388-72-3

          I. Gammel, Irene, II. Zelazo, Suzanne, III.
Title. IV. Series: Department of reissue no. ; 5

PS2919.S536C78 2010   811'.54   C2010-905586-1

TABLE OF CONTENTS

This morning
The ocean
Is just
Liquid light
Held close
And tidy
By a blue
Tulle sky
In shape
Much like
Our lace
Cake-screen.

– Florine Stettheimer

WORDS AS PAINTED AIR:

The Iridescence of Florine Stettheimer's Poetry[1]

"SHE WAS SCANDALOUS in the same way that Gertrude [Stein] was scandalous," the American composer Virgil Thomson observed of the New York poet and painter Florine Stettheimer (1871-1944), whose work has to date remained a well kept secret among aficionados of the avant-garde.[2] Virtually unknown among less specialized readers of modern poetry, the enigmatic and deeply private Stettheimer may herself be responsible for some of this neglect, having been reluctant to share, exhibit, or publicize her work. Not even her close friend, the New York writer and photographer Carl Van Vechten, was permitted to take Stettheimer's photograph, as he apologetically explained in a letter to Gertrude Stein in 1937, who had begged him to take Stettheimer's portrait for her: "Florine is NEVER photographed, Hélas! At the moment she is in Canada with ses soeurs."[3]

Yet this very elusiveness, together with Stettheimer's assumption that her poetry would never be published, may partly account for the remarkable freshness, intimacy, and frankness of the poems included herein. Stettheimer was a consummate stylist with a camp sensibility, who wrote not to please the market, but herself. Thus she granted the world only glimpses of her work, carefully choreographing and staging it for a select audience of family and friends. Emanating from a singularly private consciousness, and reveling in play and irony, her poems present a rare look at the world between the two World Wars, along with a privileged study of some of its modernist icons.

Stettheimer composed vivid and painterly poems of gently acerbic social critique. They were collected posthumously in 1949 by Stettheimer's sister Ettie and published in a private edition of 250. Intended for circulation among "Florine's friends and the friends of her paintings," the collection, entitled *Crystal Flowers*, remains little known.[4] In fact, if it were not for Barbara J. Bloemink's astute biography of the artist in 1995, which excerpts the poems as accompaniments to the narrative of Stettheimer's life, the fact that such a volume ever existed may have remained a footnote.

Our aim in re-issuing the original *Crystal Flowers* (see also Textual Note), preceded by three unpublished poems in the Prologue and followed by the libretto to her unpublished ballet "Orphée of the Quat-z-arts," is to introduce a lost modernist poet to a contemporary audience. Although Stettheimer's poetry has remained virtually unexplored for its literary merit, it invites a consideration of Stettheimer as a practitioner of an integrative, multimodal modernism that similarly characterizes the work of such avant-garde experimenters as Mina Loy, Gertrude Stein, Elsa von Freytag-Loringhoven, and Beatrice Wood. Like these modernist sisters, Stettheimer understood the power of conversation, community, and artistic consecration, cultivated in part by her role as salonière. By fusing modern elements with traditional ones, Stettheimer unleashed the full force of her artistic sensibility.

Written on scraps of paper, the poems themselves are scintillating literary gems. To early reader Mark Pagano, who had been involved with Stettheimer's exhibition at the Museum of Modern Art in 1946, the poems were "made of glass – and they have razor edges and needle points – but they have smooth velvety places to touch too."[5] This description is apt, and yet, perhaps even more accurately, the poems might be compared to sea glass: biting sharpness that has expanded, swelling to softness under the friction of waves – precision distilled until it becomes dispersive. Consider, for example, the lunar-haze of Stettheimer's aesthetic in her poem "Mother Asked": "What are you making now?/ I was sewing silver fringe/ onto stiff taffeta/ pale blue/ shot with gold/ the color of the sunglinted sea/ that was breaking/ and foaming/ below our balcony – / I answered/ I think a bathing suit/ or perhaps/ a moonwrap."

As the title *Crystal Flowers* suggests, Stettheimer's preoccupation with optical refraction – the inherent multiplicity of color contained in a single ray of light as it disperses through crystal (or any reflective material) – yields an other-worldliness, an ethereal and liminal landscape of the unconscious wherein thoughts are not yet formed, and therefore, not yet precluded. There is, instead, possibility – the possibility of movement, of atmospheric, integrative, sensory stimulation. In her poem "Sunrise" for example, sound figures as the poem's primary impetus, giving way to powerfully visual imagery, as in the evocative first lines: "The ocean is a series of contented sighs/ On it a red horizon lies."

The collection begins with nursery rhymes, but readers must not be fooled by their apparent simplicity. As they satirize the institutions of high society, the rhymes offer biting commentary on marriage, sexuality, gender roles, and the art market. The consideration of subjectivity and the lack of opportunities for the independent expression of women in Stettheimer's poem "Sweet Little Miss Mouse" presages the confessional interiority of Sylvia Plath. "Little Miss Mouse," we learn, "Wanted her own house/ So she married

Mr. Mole/ And only got a hole." The gender gap in ownership rights are here extended to the feminine voice – the mouth of the mouse fundamentally unable to articulate without the ability to *own* her own body/ house (a connection emphasized in this short poem by the phonic proximity of "mouse" to "mouth" and "house" and of course, that of "own[ing]," "Mole," and "hole.") In her poem "A Llama," Stettheimer highlights the distinctively American cycle of commodification, wherein the collector eventually becomes the collected – the Llama becoming collectible Americana, with the poet playfully riffing on the acoustic connection between "Mama" and "Americana." Significantly, "Americana" is also the title of section five in *Crystal Flowers*.

Other sections have titles such as "Nature Flora Fauna," "Things," "Comestibles," "Notes to Friends," and "As Tho' from a Diary," the latter tracing Florine's *Lehr- und Wanderjahre* in Europe and New York. Meanwhile other sections, such as "Moods" and "People," are sophisticated in evoking atmosphere and integrative immersion, and benefit the most from a juxtaposition alongside the ballet (described below).

These poems are firmly at home in interwar Manhattan, a world of "sky towers and bridal bowers/ speakeasy bars and motor cars." Thus they include references to the Upper West side, Alwyn Court, where Florine lived, and allude to Bryant Park, where she had her studio, but the poems also partake in the annual summer excursions to Asbury Park, Bedford Hills, André-Brook, Larchmont, Lake Placid, and the Jersey Coast. One of several poems entitled "New York" captures the seasonal rhythm of upper-class social life in the metropolis with haiku-like compression: "In spring my friends droop – / They disappear – / June is empty of them – / In autumn they come back/ Stuffed full of Europe." Florine's poetry interiorizes the outside world, including its popular culture, whereby references to Bendel's fashion, Walt Disney cartoons, and Broadway are juggled like the bon mots of witty conversation that enlivened her Manhattan salon. In the rooms of these poems women come and go, thinking not of Michelangelo, but of "colored balloons," "Ruffled-edge petunia leaves," "Maillard's sweets," "stiff taffeta," and "children on roller-skates." But they also think of the "steely negation" of patriarchal portrayals of women, and of the elusive connection of "spinning spiral's/ Love flight." At home in its artful, spatial interiority, Stettheimer's poetry evokes the domestic lyricism of Edith Wharton, who similarly elevated décor into literary art.

In fact, Florine and her two sisters – Ettie, a writer with a PhD in philosophy from the University of Freiburg, and Carrie, an artist, fashion plate, and conversationalist – hosted a legendary salon from 1915-

1935 for the contemporary literati, gay and polyglot New Yorkers and European expatriates. "Then we go to a party at Stettheimers," Carl Van Vechten recorded on 24 December 1926, in a typical entry in his daybook, appending a glamorous Christmas Eve guest list that reads like a *Who's Who* of Modernism: "Stella Wanger, Marcel Duchamp, the Steichens, Alfred Seligsberg, Victor Wittgenstein, Muk de Jari, Philip Moeller, Marie Sterner, Bobby & B[eatrice] Locher, Henry McBride, Best-Maugard, etc."[6] Until 1926, their salons took place at 102 West 76th Street in Manhattan, before the sisters moved to 182 West 58th Street, at Alwyn Court – what Van Vechten aptly called "Château Stettheimer," its facade adorned with salamanders and royal crowns. Containing furniture designed by Stettheimer, both homes were works of art, like the "Stetties" themselves, who adorned their bodies with artful garments and fanciful fashion.

The salon provided the raw material, and possibly a safe and contained audience, for Stettheimer's poetry. Just as she decorated the interior with her own artwork – paintings depicting her colorful guests as androgynous fauns and nymphs, so her poems offer stylized word portraiture of the era's artistic revolutionaries, many of whom openly displayed their queered sexualities in the privacy of her salon. Marcel Duchamp, the cerebral inventor of the readymade, nicknamed "Duche" in Stettheimer's eponymous poem, for example, is brilliantly captured in "A silver-tin thin spiral/ Revolving from cool twilight/ To as far as pink dawn." The visually evocative poem reads like an animation of the famous mechanomorphic drawings by Francis Picabia, himself a regular visitor at the salon, but it is also a precise verbal rendering of Florine's own 1923 painting of Marcel Duchamp sitting in an armchair and cranking up on a spiral spring the sylvan body of his female alter ego, Rrose Sélavy. Likewise, Gertrude Stein's masculine genius is playfully captured in "Gertie roared a big laugh/ ... – very male," a portrait that recalls Alice B. Toklas's comments on the baritone sensuality of Stein's voice and laughter, "deep, full, velvety, like a great contralto's, like two voices."[7] Stein famously wrote cubist word portraits of Picasso and Matisse (among others), while Stettheimer composed whimsical word paintings of Georgia O'Keeffe, Charles Demuth, Carl Van Vechten, Charles Henri Ford, Mabel Dodge and other luminaries that frequented her salon.

In all of this Stettheimer remained an observer, an outsider inviting comparisons with Emily Dickinson, whose very exile was instrumental in producing dazzling poetic innovations that anticipated modernism itself, and with whom Stettheimer shares other characteristics. Both poets dressed in white (Florine preferring white satin), flaunting nubile, sexually ambivalent personae in middle age; both defied classical traditions in art and ignored the demands of the marketplace; both coyly included some of their poems in letters to friends.[8] It might be easy to relegate Stettheimer to feminine stereotypes, casting her alternately as a Jewish-American princess, who adorns herself with expensive ornaments and fashionably artistic friends; or conversely, as "a disappointed, reclusive, virginal artist who draped her bedroom in lace and her studio in cellophane and worried that her paintings would end up in the bedroom of some unknown man."[9] However, as her biographer convincingly argues, these categories are far too reductive for the complex, if somewhat mysterious, artist. Stettheimer's privileged German-Jewish background certainly rooted her comfortably in New York's upper middle class. Born in Rochester and educated in the Art Students League of New York, as well as in Berlin, Stuttgart, and Munich, the young Florine was a cosmopolitan traveler, student, and diarist, who in 1914, at the outbreak of the First World War, permanently settled in New York with her mother and sisters. Deserted by her father early in life, Stettheimer preferred the salon life to the conventional nuclear family.

A rare photo taken of the artist in her forties (see frontispiece) shows a pensive, cerebral woman in the privacy of her Bryant Park garden, her dress blending into the floral surroundings, her modern, androgynous bob framing her angular face.[10] Duchamp affectionately called Stettheimer "a bachelor," punning on her single status and on "bachelor of the arts."[11] Like her refusal of conventional marriage and motherhood, her embrace of art was a choice. As did other empowered women artists of her generation (such as Stein, Wharton, and Willa Cather), Stettheimer came into her own in her forties, when she began to paint self-portraits in exuberant camp, depicting herself with red hair and a timeless sylvan body. Consider, for example, Stettheimer's 1915 nude *Self-Portrait*, a parodic invocation of Édouard Manet's bold-for-its-time *Olympia* (1863). Equally provocative, Stettheimer's painting depicts a nubile, rather than voluptuous body. *Self-Portrait* was a conversation stopper when Stettheimer unveiled it at one of her soirées, evidence of both her daring and her sense of humor. The painting is consistent with biographical speculation that Stettheimer exhibited "an arrested sexuality and a preference for flirtation and high-stylish affect over physical relations."[12]

Nonetheless, in Stettheimer's poetry, desire and sex are expressed in remarkably physical, if ironic, culinary metaphors that speak of a profound interest in shaping a modernist language of love and sex. "You made me hot – hot – hot/ I crisped into 'kisses,'" she writes in one poem, while claiming in another, entitled "You stirred me": "You made me giddy/ Then you poured oil on my stirred self/ I'm mayonnaise." In yet another "Comestibles" poem, she asserts: "You are consumed with longing/ For me/ La Cuisine française." Stettheimer is equally modernist in her sardonic gender critique in her poem "To a Gentleman Friend," when she exposes moments of romantic betrayal in an angry address: "You fooled me you little floating worm." Many of the poems allude to friends and artists by their initials or their first names and they are identified in the "Abbreviations and Allusions" section of this book.

There is a breezy airiness characterizing these poems, a feathery lightness, and yet the poems always contain a subversive depth revealed through wit, irony, and occasionally, a caustic bitterness. The topics revolve around the quotidian (albeit that of a distinct class) – soirées, picnics, family, friends, music and art – but they also capture a characteristically modernist iconography of self, wherein the poet teases the reader with the ironic awareness of her social role-playing, her feminine masquerade: "I turn on a soft/ Pink Light/ Which is found modest/ Even charming/ It is a protection/ Against wear/ And tears."

Working across media, indeed often at the interstice between genres (interior design, visual art, literature), Stettheimer created a fiercely independent diaphanous aesthetic, juxtaposing old-fashioned lace, taffeta and tulle with decidedly modern material such as cellophane and silver foil.[13] Her paintings, with their whimsy and innovative use of color, drawn from American industry rather than nature, as well as her figurative designs, have garnered considerable attention over the last two decades, including a retrospective at the Whitney Museum in 1995 (Marcel Duchamp had helped organize Stettheimer's first retrospective at the Museum of Modern Art in 1946 following her death). Even more recently, in 2006, Stettheimer was part of the group show "Daughters of New York DADA: Beatrice Wood, Florine Stettheimer, Clara Tice, Katherine Dreier, Mina Loy, and Baroness Elsa" at Francis M. Naumann's New York gallery.[14] Significantly, the only solo show Stettheimer had during her lifetime, which took place at the Knoedler & Company Gallery in October 1916, was a commercial disappointment. That not a single painting sold clearly compounded the artist's reticence to show publicly ever again. Ettie blamed Marie Sterner, the exhibition's curator and friend of the Stettheimer sisters. For her part, Stettheimer captures the dilettantish aspects of Sterner's curatorial forays in her poem "There's Marie Sterner." The poem concedes to Sterner's inherent talent, but hints at how it had been muted by her puppeteer-husband, in what amounts to a perspicacious critique of the dynamics of conventional marriage: "she intended to be a musician/ but Albert married her/ she learned to adore his work/ she enthusiastically/ made conversation about it."

In contrast, Stettheimer's fortuitous collaboration with Virgil Thomson and Gertrude Stein on the opera *Four Saints in Three Acts* (1934), for which Stettheimer, after a great deal of persuasion by Thomson, designed the stage set and costumes, ensured her a fair amount of critical acclaim. Stein's dissolution of scenic conventions in her libretto was mirrored by Stettheimer's creations as she adorned the stage with cellophane, palm trees, ostrich feathers and tinsel, creating other-worldly constructions that contributed to the promise of strangeness central to the opera's public appeal. With its all-black cast, *Four Saints in Three Acts* was an enormous critical and commercial success. In *Prepare for Saints*, Steven Watson points out that the show closed twice: "The first closing, on March 17, played to a packed house. The opera was already considered a success, since it had doubled the planned two-week run; not only had 45,000 people seen it, but 16,000 tickets had been sold in the final week."[15] Stettheimer's role in the production is captured in her poem for Virgil Thomson, "V.T," in which the poet intuits the experimentation of the opera as a portrait of Thomson himself. Stettheimer writes: "My role is to paint/ your four active saints/ and their props/ inside and out your portrait."

Stettheimer's libretto, "Orphée of the Quat-z-arts,

or The Revellers of the 4 Arts Ball," takes readers from New York's drawing rooms and summer resorts to the Parisian Champs Élysées. Published for the first time in its entirety in this collection, almost a full century after Stettheimer first conceived it, this ballet was inspired by the annual ball organized by the four artists' guilds in Paris. The four arts represent painting, sculpture, architecture, and literature, the very arts Stettheimer herself was drawn to.[16]

The ballet is a baccanalia of "nymphs, fauns, satyrs, bacchantes, corydons, etc.," a modern carnival that also draws on her familiarity with Munich *Fasching* and *Bals Parés* (described in her poem "Munich With Its Carnival"): "Suddenly the quiet is dispelled by music and a wild rush of revelers, artists and models coming straight from the Quat-z-arts ball, considering their joyous wild way along the Champs Elysées. *Orpheus* with his charmed lyre leads the procession." The carnival spirit with its mythological figures and artifice puts in relief Stettheimer's camp sensibilities, her way of looking at the world as "an aesthetic phenomenon," as Susan Sontag has described camp in her landmark essay "Notes on Camp." For Sontag, "Camp art is often decorative art, emphasizing texture, sensuous surface, and style at the expense of content."[17] The ballet's central character Georgette (a modern-day Euridice) navigates social strata, merging bohemian carnivalesque with the charms of "a blonde Vicomte."

Although Stettheimer's ballet was never produced, the year of its composition in 1912 marks a conceptual turning point in Stettheimer's career. Viewing Nijinsky's provocative performance in Diaghilev's Ballets Russes production of *L'Après-midi d'un Faune* was a catalyst in developing her own mature style. Diaghilev's aim to create a *Gesamtkunstwerk* (total work of art) in his production, and Nijinsky's corporeal realization of that aim cultivated Stettheimer's thinking of her work – its overall effect, atmosphere, and sensory experience – as inextricable from the setting in which it was produced. Reading Stettheimer's ballet alongside her poems, therefore, allows readers a textured experience of her poems. Thus the interdisciplinarity of Stettheimer's visual expression is tantamount to her aesthetic and yet, if she has enjoyed something of a quiet renaissance as a painter, that she also wrote poetry comes as a surprise to many – even those well-versed in her painting style and practice. This, we hope, will change with this collection.

In *Crystal Flowers* and "Orphée of the Quat-z-arts," language itself figures as a curatorial practice, the words arranged, like her floral bouquets she called "eyegays," in a deceptively simple, seemingly superficial presentation, but possessed of an emotional gravitas capable of conveying a bitingly ironic critique of her subject.[18] The artist was an adept and consistent arranger of flowers, as her numerous still-lifes attest. Similarly, one imagines that guests at the Stettheimer soirées were artfully selected to enhance the connectivity and the juxtaposition of the room. In her poetic portraits, the reader/listener is privy to a kind of private, under-her-breath disclosure of the comings and goings of high society in a reflexive, prescient observation. This dissolution of distance between creator and consumer is a central aspect of the ways in which the poems and paintings can be reciprocally enriching. Ultimately, Stettheimer's poems, like her portrait paintings for which she would construct gilt-frames, and like the ballet, for which she drew the costumes, invite the reader past the edge of the page to take a seat beside the poet. Stettheimer's work effects a perceptual permeability with the objects she depicts, gesturing beyond two-dimensionality. As Bloemink articulates: "The objects and the surrounding space interpenetrate each other. By creating an interdenominative space where objects and surfaces imperceptibly blend, Stettheimer, like Matisse, gives equal importance to the tactile and the visible, investing both with expressive meaning."[19]

In her hands, and on her tongue, the surface for Stettheimer is depth. In fact, the particular vantage point afforded the poet in part because of her highly colloquial, even conversational discourse allows her to move with ease between the cloistered high society to the carnival of the mundane, the poet cum flâneuse exploring her everyday environs with aesthetic appreciation. Among Stettheimer's notes for the ballet are mentions of the extensive research she conducted on Greek models and customs, including one likely intended to be Aphrodite but bearing an uncanny resemblance to the neo-Roman bas relief of *Gradiva*, a name that literally translates from the Latin as "the woman who walks," and who is depicted with her robes in full swing and her feet in motion.[20] With her own flowing dresses Stettheimer evokes Gradiva, but in her poems and her paintings, too, she is a Gradiva figure, walking through the American imagination, from the swing of jazz to the "beauty contests," "dance marathons/ ...and rodeos" to PT Barnum's or Walt Disney's heralding of the illusory.[21]

In 1944, Stettheimer succumbed to cancer at the age of almost 73, leaving her possessions to Carrie and Ettie. After Carrie's sudden death just six weeks later, Ettie took control of Florine's legacy, editing her sister's diaries and poetry. In November, Van Vechten wrote in a letter to Gertrude Stein: "Florine Stettheimer is dead after a brief illness and her sister Carrie followed her this summer within a month. I have been helping Ettie, the remaining sister, arrange her affairs and one of the things that has resulted is the Modern Museum has promised her a show in the fall." [22] Another fortuitous result was *Crystal Flowers*, distributed to Florine's friends in 1949. In the Foreword to her own *Memorial Volume of and by Ettie Stettheimer,* Ettie observes: "Since my sisters died, six years ago, I have spent a great deal of my time and my flagging energy in preparing their production for presentation and a chance of survival. This labour of love but also of 'psychosomatic' exhaustion has made me realize sharply that there will be no one both able and willing to do the same for me at the usual, somewhat more advanced time." She adds: "Doing for oneself has, I find, at least the one advantage for oneself in that one knows better than anyone else what it is that one wishes to accomplish. ... I want to be read widely."[23] Without diminishing Ettie's crucial editorial work – some of which is visible in the ten images of manuscripts and typescripts included herein, and is also detailed in the "Textual Notes and Endnote Annotations" section – it is important to note some of the ambivalence and tension that may have shaped her editing, and her expurgation of Florine's diaries and scrapbooks, for the relations among the "Stetties" had become more complex after their mother's death in 1935, when Florine shocked her two sisters by moving out of the communal home into her own studio.

Today that spirit of autonomy and Stettheimer's ultimate dedication to art is palpable, as her painterly poems offer further clues into a glittering pantomime of modernism. After decades-long neglect and obscurity, the iridescence of Florine's poetry is finally within the reach of readers, who are here invited to find "unexpected meanings attached to the inter-relationships of disparate words," as Marcel Duchamp wrote about poetry and puns, in which he found "an infinite field of joy."[24] We can only surmise whether or not Duchamp was privy to Stettheimer's hidden treasures, or if he was one of those strangers who felt her light was too intensive, as she writes in the aptly titled poem "Occasionally:" "A human being saw my light/ Rushed in/ Got singed/ Got scared/ .../ And when/ I am rid of/ The Always-to-be-Stranger/ I turn on my light/ and become/ myself." At the dawn of a new decade, in a new millennium, sixty years after it first appeared for a select few, Stettheimer's poetry shines for a new generation of readers ready to appreciate her irreverent camp aesthetic and her exuberant painterly style.

---

1   The title reference to "painted air" comes from Stettheimer's poem "He Photographs": "She turns them/ into painted air/ rainbowhued...."

2   Quoted in Steven Watson, *Prepare for Saints: Gertrude Stein, Virgil Thomson, and the Mainstreaming of American Modernism* (New York: Random House, 1998), 72.

3   Carl Van Vechten to Gertrude Stein, August 1, 1937, *The Letters of Gertrude Stein and Carl Van Vechten 1913-1946, vol. II* (New York: Columbia University Press, 1986), 562.

4   Ettie Stettheimer, Dedication, *Crystal Flowers* (Privately printed, 1949), [i].

5   Quoted in Barbara J. Bloemink, *The Life and Art of Florine Stettheimer* (New Haven: Yale University Press, 1995), 232.

6   Carl Van Vechten, *The Splendid Drunken Twenties: Selections from the Daybooks 1922-1930,* ed. Bruce Kellner (Urbana and Chicago: University of Illinois Press, 2003), 144. For a superb discussion of Florine Stettheimer's role as a salonière, see Emily D. Bilski and Emily Braun, "Florine Stettheimer: The Jewish Rococo," *Jewish Women and Their Salons: The Power of Conversation* (New Haven and London: Yale University Press, 2005), 126-37.

7   Alice B. Toklas, *What is Remembered* (New York: Holt Rinehard and Winston, 1963), 23.

8   For details, see Donna Graves, "'In Spite of Alien Temperature and Alien Insistence': Emily Dickinson and Florine Stettheimer," *Woman's Art Journal* 3.2 (1983), 21-7.

9   Bloemink, *Life and Art of Florine Stettheimer,* xv.

10 Reproduced in Bloemink, *Life and Art of Florine Stettheimer,* frontispiece.

11 Bilski and Braun, "Florine Stettheimer: The Jewish Rococo," 134.

12 Bloemink, *Life and Art of Florine Stettheimer,* 13.

13 See Trevor Winkfield, "Very Rich Hours – Artist Florine Stettheimer," *Art in America,* http://findarticles.com/p/articles/mi_m1248/is_n1_v84/ai_17803663/ Accessed: 11 Dec, 2009). Winkfield writes that "she was really the first true American colorist, making the big break from the European prism which by and large had been derived from nature, as opposed to Stettheimer's unearthing of American industry as a color source." See also Judith Brown, "On Cellophane," *Glamour in Six Dimensions: Modernism and the Radiance of Form* (Ithaca: Cornell University Press, 2009); Linda Nochlin, "Florine Stettheimer: Rococo Subversive," *Art in America* 68 (September 1980), 64-83; and David Tatham, "Florine Stettheimer at Lake Placid, 1919: Modernism in the Adirondacks," *The American Art Journal* 31.1 1/2 (2000), 5-31.

14 Stettheimer's second retrospective took place at the Institute of Contemporary Art in Boston in 1980. In 1990, Columbia University showcased its Stettheimer holdings, and her portraits were exhibited at the Katonah Museum of Art in 1993.

15 Watson, *Prepare for Saints,* 293.

16 For details, see Bloemink, *Life and Art of Florine*

Stettheimer, 45.

17 Susan Sontag, "Notes on Camp," *Against Interpretation and Other Essays* (New York: Farrar, Straus, and Giroux, 1966), 277-78.

18 According to Bloemink, *Life and Art of Florine Stettheimer,* 58, Stettheimer referred to her floral paintings as "'eyegays,' a word she invented to emphasize that her flowers were not for the nose but for the eye."

19 Bloemink, *Life and Art of Florine Stettheimer,* 58.

20 "Florine Stettheimer's earlier libretti etc. for her ballet 'Quatr' Art,'" Florine Stettheimer Papers, YCAL, MSS 20, Box 8, Folder 142.

21 Significantly, Sigmund Freud was himself attached to the figure of *Gradiva,* hanging a copy (rather symbolically) at the foot of his famous psychoanalytic couch, where the ambulatory gesture ushered his patients through the recesses of the unconscious mind.

22 Carl Van Vechten to Gertrude Stein, November 29, 1944, *Letters of Gertrude Stein and Carl Van Vechten 1913-1946, vol. II,* 761.

23 Ettie Stettheimer, "Foreword," *Memorial Volume of and by Ettie Stettheimer* (New York: Alfred Knopf, 1951), v.

24 Marcel Duchamp quoted in Dalia Judovitz, *Unpacking Duchamp: Art in Transit* (Berkeley: University of California Press, 1995), 90-91.

CRYSTAL FLOWERS

PROLOGUE

"[ALL MORNING]"
Manuscript, folder 134, Florine and Ettie Stettheimer Papers.
Yale Collection of American Literature, Beinecke Rare Book
and Manuscript Library

[ALL MORNING]

All morning
for hours
I have been putting flowers
together
in vases
I strip them of their green
They look more brilliant –
become more effective
"More garish" our former timid interior
decantor
Mr. B.
would have said
The bouquet I like best
I put on the dining room table
On the filet-lace round
On the light-grey painted board
It helps – It satisfies
But tomorrow
my flowers
will show the ravages of time
they will wilt
they will smell
I shall have a disgust for them
I shall dislike changing the water
And I shall feel sympathy

with Marcel
for preferring
artificial flowers

THE MASSEUSE

She lay on her bed
beneath her
spread
a pale
flower embroidered gown
the Strong one
dusted her
with fragrant powder
then took
her small foot
in a strong hand
and rubbed it
softly
then harder
then two strong hands
clutched her leg
pinched her
slapped her
pounded her
all over her fragile body

she gently sighed
and said
"You are so strong".

[I HAD BEEN LICKING IT]

I had been licking it
with the tips of my tongue
and had seen it fading away
sprinkled with tears it became my first keepsake
Other treasures followed soon
a bright hued rainbow

NURSERY RHYMES

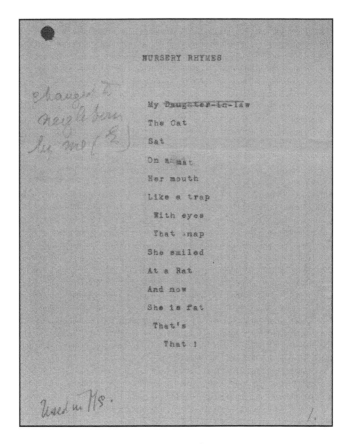

"MY NEIGHBOUR"
Typescript, folder 133, Florine and Ettie Stettheimer Papers.
Yale Collection of American Literature, Beinecke Rare Book
and Manuscript Library

[MY NEIGHBOR]

My neighbor
The Cat
Sat
On a mat
Her mouth
Like a trap
With eyes
That snap
She smiled
At a Rat
And now
She is fat
That's
That!

[MY COUSIN]

My cousin
The Rabbit
Has a queer
Habit
When asked
Why have it
She says
Dammit!

[MRS. GOLDEN-PHEASANT]

Mrs. Golden-Pheasant
looks pleasant
when she gets a present
When she gets no present
she looks unpleasant
does Mrs. Golden-Pheasant.

[THE FLAPPER]

The Flapper
The Chicken
Keeps picken'
An' picken'
It makes
Me sicken
Her everlasten'
Picken'

[A LLAMA]

A Llama
Said something
To his Mama
So she bought
A rubber mat

A brass cuspidor
And he spat. –
And now
He is collected
As Americana.

[SWEET LITTLE MISS MOUSE]

Sweet little Miss Mouse
Wanted her own house
So she married Mr. Mole
And only got a hole.

[MISS COW CALLED MISS MAISY]

Miss Cow called Miss Maisy
Murmured "I feel so lazy
I know it sounds crazy
But I should love to eat
Just one daisy".

[FAT MRS. PIGEON]

Fat Mrs. Pigeon
Full of religion
Took a walk in the park
There she met a Spark
And his remark
"What a lark"
Brought her haughty retort
"I hark
Back to the Ark"

[MR. ELEPHANT CARRIED A SPRAY OF ORANGE BLOSSOM]

Mr. Elephant carried a spray of orange blossom
in his trunk
He gave it to Miss Camel who ate it and called it
punk

[MISS BUTTERFLY]

Miss Butterfly
Sighed a sigh
"My name does me belie
I shall change it to Flutterby

For I love the air
And to flutter
And I do not care
For butter"

[A FOOLISH LIZZARD]

A foolish Lizzard
Ran into a blizzard
So he continued to run
Like fun
For the Sun.

[MR. TANGO EEL]

Mr. Tango Eel
has no heel –
and as for hair
it's very rare –
he cannot shave
his permanent wave

[MISS LOVEY DOVE]

Miss Lovey Dove
Did prettily coo
I expect my love
To come me to woo
Up into the sky
I shall fly
There I may sigh
To him
Aye aye.

[THE DINOSAUR]

The Dinosaur
Was very big
And devoured many
A luscious fig
He left the leaves
To Adam and Eve
And the Greek Gods
To wear or to leave

[QUEER MR. BAT]

Queer Mr. Bat
Finds day-life flat
So he hangs by his toes
And sees with his nose.

["WHY SHOULD I CARE"]

"Why should I care"
With his sardonic air
Young Leopard growls
At night when he prowls
"If I have one spot
Or a whole lot –
Like many a mate
I know my fate
On a future cold day
In the U.S.A.
I shall be a sack
Worn on the back
On a thin girl or fat
With an Alice-blue hat."

THE ZOO

Said the Kangaroo
"I just love the Zoo
For I've nothing to do
Isn't that true?"

Said the Chimpanzee
"I wish to be free
And sit on a tree
When it suits me!"

Said the Bear
"It's not fair
For we lose our hair
And it's hard to repair."

[I LIKE THE AIR]

I like the air
when sunny
I like flowers
with honey
said the Bee.

I like people

full of blood
and the world
full of mud
said the Flea.

[YOUNG ARTIST RAT]

Young Artist Rat
In a garret sat
Caught in a trap
"I'm a modern chap
For the funnel
I took for a tunnel
And the dead fish
I thought smelt delish
I shall paint in cubes
And call it Prudes
And add a rotten banana
In my very best manner."

[ALL SHE OWNED]

All she owned
Was a white fur coat
And a white curly pom

So she stood on the street
On her velvet silk feet
And waited for something to come

NATURE • FLORA • FAUNA

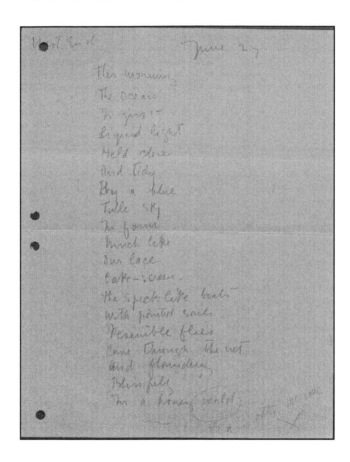

"THIS MORNING"

Manuscript, folder 134, Florine and Ettie Stettheimer Papers.
Yale Collection of American Literature, Beinecke Rare Book
and Manuscript Library

SUNRISE

The ocean is a series of contented sighs
On it a red horizon lies
The birds are chirping expectantly

The world is growing lighter
And the birds quieter

Out of the sea came
A ball of flame

It has burst into light
The world is bright

The bird-claque is hushed
Worms are being crushed.

[THE SUN]

The sun
Is teasing
The sea
Throwing darts
Of light
On the crests of waves

Goading them
Higher
And higher
Until dazzled
They overbalance
And dissolve in foam.

[THIS MORNING]

This morning
The ocean
Is just
Liquid light
Held close
And tidy
By a blue
Tulle sky
In shape
Much like
Our lace
Cake-screen.
The speck-like boats
With pointed sails
Resemble flies
Come through
The net

And floundering
Blissfully
In a honey-sea.

[ROBINS HOP]

Robins hop
Fleas hop
Flappers hop
They never stop

Lindbergh hops
Chamberlain hops
Byrd hops
All non-stops

THE OCEAN

I the silver moon
attract you
repulse you
upheave you
subside you
move you
calm you

eternally enslave you

I the golden sun
make you glitter
make you sparkle
make you colorful
make you gorgeous
leave you indifferent

[THE RAINBOW SHED]

The rainbow shed
Diamond tears
On the pinky white roses
And changed them
From usualness
To frivolous glittering
Posies
And the elm tree beyond
Is all aglitter too
And would be
A lovely fan
For you

SPRING

I just woke up
Spring must have come
Birds are twittering
The way they would
When little green things
Come out of the ground
And little red things
Bud out of trees
And little yellow things
Blossom out of shrubs
There's titivating
There's titillating
Spring's all aflitter
Spring's all atwitter.

[I PLANTED GREENY-WHITE PETUNIAS]

I planted greeny-white Petunias
They developed magenta streaks
My pink ones got black centers
And I have many other freaks

My Lady-slippers were flesh color
They turned into deep rose red

Because some vermilion Zinnias
Were alongside in the same bed

My pale Dahlia watched my Sunflower
Which in turn kept watching the sun
The Dahlia turned a queer yellow
Does the Sunflower see the fun?

BREAKFAST TIME
André-Brook

I am lying in bed
My balcony door is open
The sun is shining
There's a yellow bird
In the elm tree –
It chirped –
An orange bird
Has joined it –
A green caterpillar
Has changed beaks
Been flown away with

Aroma of coffee
Aline is bringing my breakfast
I'm glad it's not a caterpillar –

THE REVOLT OF THE VIOLET

This is vulgar age
Sighed the violet
Why must humans drag us
Into their silly lives
They treat us
As attributes
As symbols
And make us
Fade
Stink

[I HAVE HUNG]

I have hung
My moonstones
On my zebra's
Ears
I put a wreath
Of Zinnias
Round his neck
I fed to him
The Portulaca
And threw
The Petunias

To his feet
I held the morning glory
In my hand
It is a heavenly blue
And whispered
To my decked out pet
This flower
Is not
For you.

[TODAY]

Today
The breaking waves
Look like
Ruffled-edge petunia leaves

[OUR PRIVET HEDGES ARE IN BLOOM]

Our privet hedges are in bloom
And the outdoor world
Is like a fragrance-laden
Room

THE FLUTTERBY

I saw a flutterby die…
It was on Easter Sunday morning
in my white and gold bed-room
overlooking the Tuilleries gardens…
It must have been hidden away
in a bunch of lilies
out of which it limply fluttered
to the high sunny balcony window
and then swooned…
I tried to revive it
I sent Jeanne for the honey jar
I sent Jeanne for the sugar bowl
but the flutterby crawled
over my sky-blue satin couvre-lit
spread its yellow wings
and did an unbeautiful act
… It died …

[MOSQUITOES BITE]

Mosquitoes bite
I know
I don't bite
Do mosquitoes know

When do mosquitoes sleep
I don't know
When I sleep
Mosquitoes know

ASTERS

You degoute me
You tame
Purple
Pink
White
Asters –
Black Beetles
Crawl
All over you –
When I step on one of your Shiny Bugs
And burst it open
It is full of you

You tame
Purple
Pink
White
Asters –

[OUR FANCY PET]

Our fancy pet
The Zebra
Is munching
Niggertoes
He has a bed
Of cat-tails
And ambered musk
For his nose

A DANCE

The Banana trees
Sway in the breeze
This way
They sway
They sway
This way

The bananas drop
From the tree top

They drop
And they flop
They flop
When they drop

[THE FIREFLIES ARE EATEN UP]

The fireflies are eaten up
The bats look debonair
Like aeroplanes they fuel up
When on the wing in midair

ADVENTURE IN LARCHMONT

Scaredly cackling the stray white hen
Hopped up the steps of the kitchen stoop
Chased by a sleek green-eyed cat –
I saved the chicken from attack
Altho' my taste was that of the cat.

THE DOVES

The sun is setting
And the moon is rising
In the opalescent sky
Two birds are fluttering
In ever widening circles
Up high.
The white dove
And the purple one
Rested on the red brick church
Then soaring into
The moon region
There seemed to end their search.

For I saw them drop
Into a celadon-green tree top.

EPHEMÈRE

I broke the glistening spider web
That held a lovely ephemère
I freed its delicate legs and wings
Of all the sticky untidy strings
It stayed with me a whole summer's day
Then it simply flew away –

THINGS

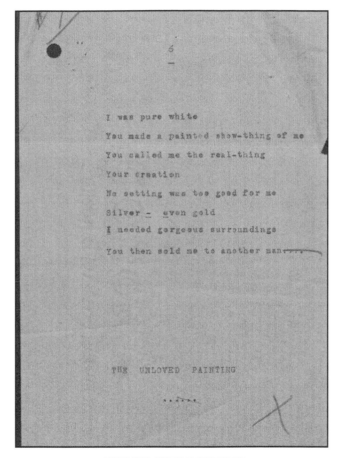

6
—

I was pure white
You made a painted show-thing of me
You called me the real-thing
Your creation
No setting was too good for me
Silver - even gold
I needed gorgeous surroundings
You then sold me to another man

THE UNLOVED PAINTING

"THE UNLOVED PAINTING"
Typescript, folder 135, Florine and Ettie Stettheimer Papers.
Yale Collection of American Literature, Beinecke Rare Book
and Manuscript Library

[MY ATTITUDE IS ONE OF LOVE]

My attitude is one of love
is all adoration
for all the fringes
all the color
all tinsel creation

I like slippers gold
I like oysters cold
and my garden of mixed flowers
and the sky full of towers
and traffic in the streets
and Maillard's sweets
and Bendel's clothes
and Nat Lewis hose
and Tappé's window arrays
and crystal fixtures
and my pictures
and Walt Disney cartoons
and colored balloons

THE UNLOVED PAINTING

I was pure white
You made a painted show-thing of me
You called me the real-thing
Your creation
No setting was too good for me
Silver – even gold
I needed gorgeous surroundings
You then sold me to another man

MY HANDKERCHIEF

A tiny
Filmyedged
Square of linen
Was waving
In the moonlight
All last night
In the yard
Where the three
Trees of Heaven
Make a pattern
Against the sky
With other wraith-like companions
It was hung

From a line
To be bleached
By the moon
To whiteness
And now
All perfumed lightness
It's being pressed
To Paulet's lips.

THERMOS BOTTLE
The Death Explosion

It was pink in the days
when I painted the picnic
under the willows
in Bedford Hills
Later I gold-leafed it
to match my bedroom
in the Alwyn Court
in town
It had a long life
fifteen years
Until last night
in the sweltering heat
our German Marie
stuffed it full of ice

and brought it to me
a poor shattered thing
With a righteous look
on her stubborn face
with finality she said
"id have explodiert"

[I FOUND PINK HEARTS]

I found pink hearts
soft to the touch
stuffed with fragrance
nestling among her underthings
I gently stole one
jammed it
full of pins
and hung it up
    my Saint Sebastian.

[MOTHER ASKED]

Mother asked
What are you making now?
I was sewing silver fringe
onto stiff taffeta

pale blue
shot with gold
the color of the sunglinted sea
that was breaking
and foaming
below our balcony –
I answered
I think a bathing suit
or perhaps
a moonwrap

[ART IS SPELLED WITH A CAPITAL A]

Art is spelled with a capital A
And capital also backs it
Ignorance also makes it sway
The chief thing is to make it pay
In a quite dizzy way
Hurrah – hurrah –

COMESTIBLES

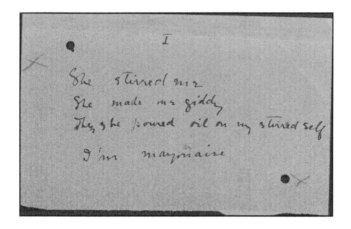

"SHE STIRRED ME"
Manuscript, folder 136, Florine and Ettie Stettheimer Papers.
Yale Collection of American Literature, Beinecke Rare Book
and Manuscript Library

[YOU BEAT ME]

You beat me
I foamed
Your sweetest sweet you almost drowned me in
You parcelled out my whole self
You thrust me into darkness
You made me hot – hot – hot
I crisped into "kisses"

[YOU ARE ROUGH]

You are rough
You punch me
You make me roll
How do you want me?
I am your clay
I am pliable
I lie soft in your hands
Mold me

You threw me aside
Then understanding
I knew how
I grew big
I became shapeless

You came back
Your eyes saw me

You treated me to hellfire
You kept close watch on me
For I am now precious to you
Your golden loaf
Your daily bread

[YOU STIRRED ME]

You stirred me
You made me giddy
Then you poured oil on my stirred self
I'm mayonnaise

[YOU CALLED ME A PEACH]

You called me a peach
Nevertheless you cut me
You called me luscious beauty
Nevertheless you cut me
I know you loved me
Yet you continued to cut me
Cruel one

Then I found you loving my sisters
One you called Downy-Cheeks
One you called Peachy-Skin
Another Ripe-Sweetness
Nevertheless you cut us all

We fell into an inert heap
We drooped into each other
Our life sap oozed from us
We faded
You forgot us

Again you came our way
No longer were we your pretties
We were wilting and yellowing
Insult and scorn you heaped upon us
You appraised us with
"Cream might improve you
Also some sugar"

STUFFED PEPPERS

Your sharpness
Brings tears to my eyes
And only
When I have dug through
To your inner softness
I breathe freely once more

[YOU CALLED ME HOG]

You called me hog
You took me in hand
You cured me with sweetness
You gave me taste
You changed me completely
Even my name
You called me Ham

CHAUD-FROID

You are hot
You are cold
Your black beauty spots
Enhance your creamy whiteness

You are delicious
You are a dream
You are full of softness
Full of delicacies
Marvelously blended
I gloat over your perfections
And voluptuously destroy you –
You wonderful hot-cold thing

TOMATOES RUSSIAN DRESSING

Your Russian style of dressing
Becomes you
Is delicious
You Jersey country product –
I adore
Your native flatness
I am wild
Over your acquired pep

TO P.

Paul you are my Valentine
You have a passion for me
Because you ignored me

For six long months
You look haggard
Your eye is wild
You are emaciated
You pine for me
My memory gives you no peace
Night and day you think of me
You are consumed with longing
For me

      La Cuisine française

AMERICANA

New York

In spring my friends droop-
They disappear -
June is empty of them -
In autumn they come back
Stuffed full of Europe.

"NEW YORK"
Typescript, folder 137, Florine and Ettie Stettheimer Papers.
Yale Collection of American Literature, Beinecke Rare Book
and Manuscript Library

NEW YORK

In spring my friends droop –
They disappear –
June is empty of them –
In autumn they come back
Stuffed full of Europe.

FLOWER SHOW

The Flower Show looked
like an expensive funeral
On the formal grass plots
stood scentless flowers
Expressionless dumb beefy men
stood in attendance
A white haired bearded visitor
with hatless bent head
whispered to his hushed companion

Who were all the buried?

[WHY CALL THEM]

Why call them
Movie stars

I call them
Movies torches
and on occasions
pronounce it
tortures

PROHIBITION

Version 1
A blimpity blimp
Was a little way up
A voice called from earth
"Hey there stop!

I know you have wine
Send down a line
I'll come up
I'm a revenue cop"

"Come along up
But if you look
There's a parachute"

Version 2
A blimpity blimp
Soared over my house

A voice called down
"Do you want to souse

Three miles up
And we'll carouse
Be a sport
I have some port

If I don't suit
There's a parachute"

Version 3
A blimpity blimp
Was right above
A soft voice called
"You are a love
One mile up
And we will sup
And I'm alert
If you want to flirt

And if I don't suit
There's the parachute"

ASBURY PARK

It swings
it rings
it's full of noisy things

It's stretched
along the water
on a boardwalk

Hurray
We are gay
is what the crowds say
lying stretched on land
along the water's sand

[IN THE MUS-E-UM]

In the Mus-e-um
The Directors drink Rum
For Art is dumb
In the Mus-e-um.

[THE HAPPY BRIDE DROPPED ALL]

The happy bride dropped all
her clothes
Then powdered her broad
but delightful nose
"An dis is what for is
my bridal veil
Covering me all up
I look quite pale"
Chuckled blissfully dusky
black Rose

[MARY, MARY OF THE]

Mary, Mary of the
Bronx aerie
How does your V garden
Grow
With beans and potatoes
Peas and tomatoes
And shiny bugs all in a
Row

MOODS

"A GOLDEN GOD"
Manuscript, folder 138, Florine and Ettie Stettheimer Papers.
Yale Collection of American Literature, Beinecke Rare Book
and Manuscript Library

[THIS SUMMER IS GONE]

This summer is gone
I did not live it –
I killed time
It was like swatting flies
The hours fell dead
Noiselessly –
I did not ever hear them buzz
I had no flowers –
Others had a few –
There were big trees
But they belonged to nobody –

Then we drove South-west
Over smooth roads –
That way we got ahead of time –

It's September now –
Children on roller skates
Are gratingly rolling over time –
I shall soon roll on wheels
Back to town
To take up time
And again become over-aware
Of its preciousness –

[I'M TIRED]

I'm tired
My sobs
rise
like
bubbles
in a syphon

[OCCASIONALLY]

Occasionally
A human being
Saw my light
Rushed in
Got singed
Got scared
Rushed out
Called fire
Or it happened
That he tried
To subdue it
Or it happened
He tried to extinguish it
Never did a friend
Enjoy it

The way it was
So I learned to
Turn it low
Turn it out
When I meet a stranger –
Out of courtesy
I turn on a soft
Pink light
Which is found modest
Even charming
It is a protection
Against wear
And tears
And when
I am rid of
The Always-to-be-Stranger
I turn on my light
And become myself

TO A GENTLEMAN FRIEND

You fooled me you little floating
worm
For I looked for the wings
With which you seemed to fly
And make you different

From other worms
And then I discovered the slender
thread
That fastened you safely to a solid tree
I touched the thread
With my finger tip
And you wiggled
I snapped the thread and you fell to
earth
And you squirmed
And wormed
And only wiggled

NARCISSUS

You play in my garden
You are very young
You are beautiful
You see in the red rambler arches
Frames for your posturing
In the fullblown peony borders
Boundaries for your dance
In the smooth lawn
A carpet for you somersaults
In the clear pool
Yourself reflected

In my eyes
Your selfworshipped self idolized

A GOLDEN GOD

I adore men sunkissed and golden
Like gold gods
Like Pharaoh amber-anointed
Thus I mused aloud
Lying on a lace-cushioned-couch
On my veranda overhanging Lake
Placid –
My August-guest
Heard me and smiled
And rose lazily from the turkey-red
Cushions
He became a golden speck
Paddling into the blazing sun
Hours later he came back
Looking self-conscious and parboiled

LOVE POEM

I invited you much
often

all the time
You only came sometimes
You fatuously smiled
and said
"Propinquity is necessary to Love
you think?"
I demurely said
"Perhaps"
You never suspected
I only loved you
when absent.

[OH HORRORS]

Oh horrors
I hate Beethoven
And I was brought up
To revere him
Adore him
Oh horrors
I hate Beethoven

I am hearing the Fifth Symphony
Led by Stokowski
It's being done heroically
Cheerfully pompous

Insistently infallible
It says assertively
Ja – Ja – Ja –
Jawohl – Jawohl
Pflicht – Pflicht
Jawohl
Herrliche Pflicht
Deutsche Pflicht
Ja – Ja – Ja – Ja –
And heads nod
In the German way
Devoutly affirmative
Oh horrors
And now
Pianissimo
And firmly tender
So – So – So – So –
Jaso – Jaso
Gut – Gut
And heads nod
In the German way

Piously ecstatic
Oh horrors
I hate Beethoven.

[YOU REMIND ME]

You remind me
of a follower
who adores me
who bores me

If you adored me
would you bore me
I shall wonder
forever

[A GOLDEN YOUTH]

A golden youth
Sat under a tree
A silver fish
Swam in the sea

A golden youth
Swam in the sea
A silver fish
Hung on a tree

A golden youth
Lay under a tree

A silver fish
Was inside he

[A FRIEND DIED]

A friend died
he left an empty world to me
it is so big
and so desolate
I want to get rid of it
to whom could I give it
I shall stay in my studio

I may forget it.

[YOU ARE THE STEADY RAIN]

You are the steady rain
The looked-fors
The must-bes
The understandables
The undistinguishables
The inevitables
The earthmoisteners
The great mud makers

We are the sunbursts
We turn rain
Into diamond fringes
Black clouds
Into pink tulle
And sparrows
Into birds of Paradise

THE 13TH OF OCTOBER

A black butterfly
with a long black shadow
was there
in my room
when I switched on the light
In the very middle
planted
on my coppercolored carpet…
It was motionless
it looked permanent
it thrilled me
with horror…
The grey walls
grew icy
the Japanese prints

did harakiri…
In my chill terror I make a vow:
I shall do my room
in white and gold
and paint gay flowers
on the walls
and honey bees
and white butterflies
and the song of birds
and the sun's bright rays!

[FOR A LONG TIME]

For a long time
I gave myself
To the arrested moment
To the unfulfilled moment
To the moment of quiet expectation
I painted the trance moment
The promise moment
The moment in the balance
In mellow golden tones…
Then I saw
Time
Noise
Color

Outside me

Around me

Knocking me

Jarring me

Hurting me

Rousing me

Smiling

Singing

Forcing me in joy to paint them …

PEOPLE

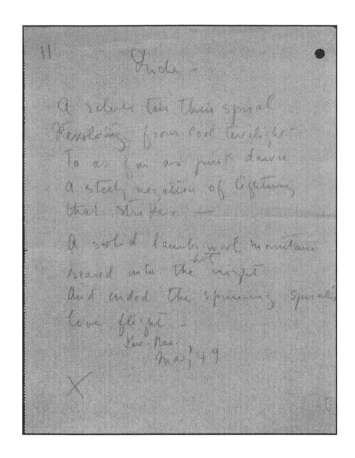

"DUCHE"

[CARL]

Carl
Carlo
Carl Van Vechten
There is Fania
There is Peter
There is Mabel
There is Edna
There are cats
Past cats
Present cats
Future cats
There is music –
However
There are
Carl
Carlo
Carl Van Vechten

[HE PHOTOGRAPHS]

He photographs.
She is naked
he proclaims
She has no clothes

other than his words.
Goldenbrown and autumnred
they drop fast
and cyclone about her

She turns them
into painted air
rainbowhued
that whirls and swirls
and sucks him in

C.D.

Charles is concocting
a pudding
Of Georgia
Peggy
Florine
Of Pomegranates
Persimmons
Whipped Cream

Georgia the smooth icing
Peggy the tart spicing
The Angelica trim
Florine

TO PHYLLIS

I am Citronella, Phyllis
My tragedy is
You do not need me
I would anoint you
Against winged evils
That surround you
By day
At night
Alas
You are invulnerable, Phyllis
That is Citronella's tragedy

[GERTIE MET A UNICORN]

Gertie me a Unicorn
It was black and waved
its tail
Gertie roared a big laugh
back – very male

P.T.

Your show at the Museum
is overwhelmingly you
your mountainous thoughts
your fountainous talk
your leafy gestures
Are you keeping
your skyey laughter
and flowery accolades
for paradise

DUCHE

A silver-tin thin spiral
Revolving from cool twilight
To as far as pink dawn
A steely negation of lightning
That strikes

A solid lamb-wool mountain
Reared into the hot night
And ended the spinning spiral's
Love flight –

V.T.

The thrush in our elm tree top
has been singing questions
for days
I feel clarified
This is my clarification
My role is to paint
your four active saints
and their props
inside and out your portrait
St Gertrude will protect you all

[THERE'S MARIE STERNER]

There's Marie Sterner
she intended to be a musician
but Albert married her
she learned to adore his work
she enthusiastically
made conversation about it
Albert doted on her
Albert swore by her
Albert cherished her greatly
Marie had much charm
which she could not hide forever

behind Albert's pictures
 – Other artists
wanted
themselves
and
their
work
adored by Marie

J.S.

He came to my studio
He had begged
"It's years since I've been
I'm crazy to see your paintings
I love to chat with you
I adore having tea with you."
He bores me
I let him come
I gave him tea
I did not chat
He did some chatting
Then suddenly I heard
"You have a superiority complex"
And I never knew it –
So it was funny after all.

[YOU DID US MUCH HARM]

You did us much harm
bearded Herr Frommer
Your brown eyes
had a kindly look
You had so many children
You came to us often
knelt before each one of us
measured our young feet
and made shoes
that did not fit them
You occasioned us
much suffering
which we have never forgotten
kindly eyed bearded Herr Frommer.

[WE FLIRTED]

We flirted
In New York
On the Jersey Coast
In Paris
On the Riviera
In Munich
In the Engadine

For years and years
"I am sailing
for home
on the Rotterdam."
"I am booked
on the Majestic."
"Quel Malheur!"
We flirted
On the Rotterdam
We passed the Narrows
Flirting
We passed French Liberty
Flirting
"Let's celebrate
this faithful
long flirtation
give a fête
invite many
They shall give us
Crystal things
Diamonds
Venetian glass
Perhaps
we could accept
Sapphires
Perhaps
we could build

a treasure house
all of glass."
His glasses
strangely
dulled
his eyes
They became
An opaque barrier
on which
Our flirtation
Shattered
In a thousand
Splinters.

ON A VERANDA

You are invulnerable, Phyllis
I bit you
You did not move an eyelash
I am almost bursting
I have Latin blood in me
Your neighbours', Phyllis

[THE WORLD IS FULL OF STRANGERS]

The world is full of strangers
They are very strange
I am never going to know them
Which I find easy to arrange

[LOOK AT MY]

Look at my
painting
look at my
painting
cried the boy
Groaned the
public
go play with a
toy

[THEY LIKE A WOMAN]

They like a woman
to have a mind
they are of greater interest
they find

They are not very young
women of that
kind

[TAME LITTLE KISSES]

Tame little kisses
one must give
to Uncles Nephews
and Nieces
And to friends
who say you are charming
one does likewise
nothing alarming

NOTES TO FRIENDS

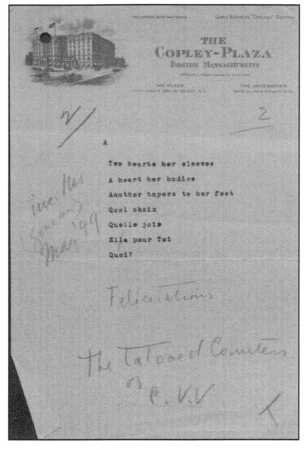

"TO CARL VAN VECHTEN"
Typescript, folder 140, Florine and Ettie Stettheimer Papers.
Yale Collection of American Literature, Beinecke Rare Book
and Manuscript Library

[DEAR CARLO]

Dear Carlo
I am agitated
It's so sudden
so unexpected
bound up with you
for life
chained
cobwebbed
a difference
an indifference
Would you coldly undedicate us
I am agitated
Dear Carlo

                    Florine

CARLO

                    Colorful scents
                    Scented rhythms
                    Rhythmic flavors
                    Flavorful discords
                    Discordant youth
                    Youthless gaiety
                    Gay degeneration

You created
for greeneyed Campaspe to her delight

———————————————

to my amazement

My thanks

TO CARL VAN VECHTEN

Two hearts her sleeves
A heart her bodice
Another tapers to her feet
Quel choix
Quelle joie
Elle a pour Toi
Quoi?

Felicitations

HOUPLA CARLO!

American youth
will stand
on
one another's heads

and clap
their feet
in your honor!
You struck
a mighty blow
for our deliverance
from our
National Pest.
May all
Nature Dancers
curl all their pinkies
and droop – droop –
to earth
and never rise again.
My thanks!

TO CARL

Darling Moses
Your Black Chillun
Are floundering
In the sea

Gentle Moses
The waves don't part
To let us

Travel free

Holy Moses
Lead us on
To Happyland
To any land with thee

TO DICK

This morning
Your gift came naked
Waxy-pink cushioned on green
Its softness enhanced
By drops of ruby blood –
Tonight
Anointed with cinnamon
Cloves and oil
And purified by fire
It was rushed to its doom

[I TRIED TO DISSECT THE MARZIPAN HEART]

I tried to dissect the Marzipan heart
The smooth surface bent the steel
Foiled – I let it drop.

It will go into Lina's mill
Be ground to sweet powder
Strewn on our Sunday tart
I shall eat your heart.

TO PHILIP

When I got to my studio
This beautiful May morning
Your Sophie was there
You sent her to me
She is mine
I removed her blue wrap
Her cerulean trimmed
Lemon underthing
Was like spring
She did not look
Her best
On my Venetian-red
Cushioned couch.
But oh
How lovely
On my black
Gold-fringed
Rug.

TO DAVID P.

What a beautiful cane
What a sturdy support
What a good sort!
Never need to fall again

DEAR POET
Charles Henri Ford

Did the lake overturn
when Narcissus fell in
become opaque
a mad lake –
Oh poet dear
please make it clear
and let it recover
the reflected image
of that foolish lover –

Amazedly

Florine St.

AS THO' FROM A DIARY

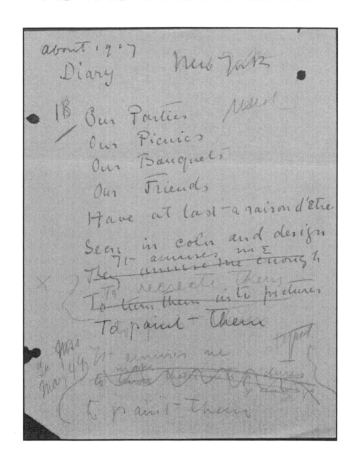

[A PINK CANDY HEART]

A pink candy heart
In fluted tin
A spun glass rainbow
On a lace paper sky
A toy peacock
That spread its tail
A first beau's picture
With glossy curls
Were early cherished treasures

[MY RING FELL FROM THE NURSERY WINDOW]

My ring fell from the nursery window
into a flower bed below
A fairy hopped out of a waterlily
in a Xmas Pantomime Show
Maggie carried me into a circus
to give the little rider a kiss
In our oleandertreed yard on a stage
I sang 'little Maggie May' with bliss
I dressed up in paper muslin
with gold fringes and gold stars
in that golden era when to
adventures there were no bars

AND THINGS I LOVED –

Mother in a low-cut dress
Her neck like alabaster
A laced up bodice of Veronese green
A skirt all puffs of deeper shades
With flounces of point lace
Shawls of Blonde and Chantilly
Fichues of Honeton and Point d'Esprit
A silk jewel box painted with morning glories
Filled with ropes of Roman pearls
Mother playing the Beautiful Blue Danube
We children dancing to her tunes
Embroidered dresses of white Marseilles
Adored sashes of pale watered silk
Ribbons with gay Roman stripes
A carpet strewn with flower bouquets
Sèvres vases and gilt console tables
Mother reading us fairy tales
When sick in bed with childhood ills –
All loved and unforgettable thrills

[SCHOOLDAYS IN A PRETTY TOWN]

Schooldays in a pretty town
Where lived a King and Queen

And Papageno and Oberon
Goetz and Lohengrin
There was a military band
To which we "Little Ones" paraded
With Maggie every day at noon
And a cakestore which we raided
Every day at four
And life was full of parties
In woods where wildflowers grew
In parks where Greek Gods postured
In our parlor of tufted Nattier blue

FIRST PLASTIC ART – HERR GOTT

Sh – Sh – shushed Maggie
Sprinkling holy water in my face
On entering the little chapel
From the sunny village street

In the light of the tall window
An enormous statue stood
A man in a purple gown
With a high golden crown

He had very pink cheeks
And a long white beard

And his hand was raised in blessing

Maggie knelt and pulled me down
Crossing herself she loudly whispered
"That is the Lord God
With the golden crown"

[IN BERLIN]

In Berlin
I went to school
I painted
I skated
I adored gay uniforms
I thought they contained superforms
Though they did not quite conform
To my beauty norm
The Belvedere Apollo

[ART STUDENT DAYS IN NEW YORK]

Art student days in New York
Streets of stoop-houses all alike
People dressed sedately
Bright colours considered loud

Jewels shoddy
I affected Empire gowns
Had an afternoon at home
Attended balls and parties
At Sherrys and Delmonicos
Sat through operas and the
Philharmonic
I had a friend who looked Byronic
With whom I discussed books
Emerson and Ruskin
Mills and Henry James
When we felt mild
When we felt ironic
It was Whistler and Wilde

[IN NEW YORK]

In New York
Cows
Sheep
Even chickens
Hang
In heavily gilt ornate frames
On your
Old rose
Satin brocade walls

You live
Sedately
Dignifiedly
With your treasured costly cattle
portraits
They replace ancestors
Even flowers
Pompous
Bearded
Painters
Painted them
Pompous
Picture dealers
Sold them to you
In red plush sanctums
Cows
Sheep
Even Pigs
Watch you
Sit
Satisfiedly
On gilt velvet-tufted chairs.

[ROME WITH STREETS OF PALACES]

Rome with streets of palaces
Villas and Roman baths
Diplomats and savanti
Archaeologists and galanti
Litterati and padri
Camellias and olive trees
Battaglie de Fiori
Music on the Pincio
Magnolias and fireflies
Dreaming in the Villa d'Este
Having pearls put in my hair
By a painter who proclaimed me
Not unlike Pinturicchio damosels fair

[PARIS – LIVING IN THE LATIN QUARTER]

Paris – living in the Latin Quarter
And flanéing in the Bois
Going to staid dinner parties
In Callot gowns chez moibored by
my painting master
Rather charmed by a blond Vicomte
Approving of French tools
Also of French Art

Thrilled by the Russian Ballet
And cakes made by Rebattet
Liking Marquis chocolate
And petits pois à la française

[MUST ONE HAVE MODELS]

Must one have models
must one have models forever
nude ones
draped ones
costumed ones
"The Blue Hat"
"The Yellow Shawl"
"The Patent Leather Slippers"
Possibly men painters really
need them – they created them

[MUNICH WITH ITS CARNIVAL]

Munich with its carnival
Rosenkavalier Parzival
Künstler Feste Bals Parés
Satisfying my costume craze –
The gay youths had chic ways

And fortunately fantastic arrays
And I tried many a new painting medium
Which prevented any tedium.

[CASEIN WAS ONCE MILK]

Casein was once milk
And then it was cheese
And now it is pictures
   How wonderful
At noon came my 'Meister'
In white tie and tails
To look at my work
   How wonderful
Casein looks like fresco
And Herr Apotheker F. said
"red vill last foreffer"
   How vonterfool
I shall paint the walls
For tout New York
On my return
   Most wonderful

[THEN BACK TO NEW YORK]

Then back to New York
And skytowers had begun to grow
And front stoop houses started to go
And life became quite different
And it was as tho' someone had planted seeds
And people sprouted like common weeds
And seemed unaware of accepted things
And did all sorts of unheard of things
And out of it grew an amusing thing
Which I think is America having its fling
And what I should like is to paint this thing.

[PRIMITIVE SAINTS]

Primitive Saints
Renaissance Prophets
Even Gothic Madonnas
Hang on your Genoese velvet walls
You live modernly
Cocktailedly
With your costly Old Masters
They replace
Ancestors
Flowers

Youths of their times painted them
Youths of our time copy them
Picture merchants
Sell them to you
In red plush sanctums
Saints
Madonnas
Even Martyrs
Watch you
Jazz
Gayly
Giddily
On shiny waxed floors

NEW YORK

At last grown young
with noise
and color
and light
and jazz
dance marathons and poultry shows
soulsavings and rodeos
gabfeasts and beauty contests
sky towers and bridal bowers
speakeasy bars and motor cars
columnists and movie stars

[WHICH –]

Which –
How can I choose
So many
So much
New York's make up
Sky towers
May parties
Summer Beaches
Beauty contests
Broadway's lights
Movie Cathedrals
Dance Marathons
And Rodeos
Shriners Parades
Soul Savers
And Horse Shows

[OUR PARTIES]

Our Parties
Our Picnics
Our Banquets
Our Friends
Have at last a raison d'être

Seen in color and design
It amuses me
To recreate them
To paint them.

ORPHÉE OF THE QUAT-Z-ARTS

OR

THE REVELLERS OF THE 4 ARTS BALL

Paris

moonlight – dawn – morning.

The Champs Elysées.

It is a starlit mild Spring night. The dark Chestnut trees are in blossom. The blossoms shine like white candles. Behind the great trees, to the right of the stage, are seen the lights of the restaurant "Les Ambassadeurs." Tables are on the lawn which also is studded and festooned with lights – at *two* of them belated guests are seated.

One couple rises from their table, the gentleman helps the lady with her wrap, takes his hat and cane from the waiter, they depart. One other couple remains at a table enjoying the night and their absinthe.

The tired waiters lean up against the trees.

From the left an apache and his girl come in, fooling and playing with one another, a short dispute whether to stay or go in follows and ends in their sitting in immobile embrace, on a bench on the roadside.

The last couple now rises from their table and depart.

Only one tired waiter remains who seats himself.

A fat porter comes out of the restaurant and turns off various switches on the lawn – and the lights go out –

He returns to the restaurant and the lights there go out. The night becomes quiet and dark, – some pedestrians pass along the Champs Elysées, quietly, homeward bound.

Some traffic –

Two vegetable carts on their way to market – , the drivers atop asleep – the horses walking as if in their sleep.

Complete silence of the dead of night.

– Suddenly the quiet is dispelled by music and a wild rush of revelers, artists and models coming straight from the Quat-z-arts ball, considering their joyous wild way along the Champs Elysées. *Orpheus* with his charmed lyre leads the procession. Among his wild followers are nymphs, fauns, satyrs, bacchantes, corydons, etc – animals

Orpheus dances, his followers take up the dance and it becomes a wild bacchanalia –

In the meantime the more slovenly moving part of the cortège arrives, representing gods, godesses, animals etc – livened by Orpheus' music –

(This part is a procession arranged in organic groups, each one of which enters by itself to make a complete picture, before the succeeding one comes on. Most of these groups do dances)

1st group. Euridice and her snake (she does a snake dance

    the apache fascinated, drawn to her dances.)

2nd Aphrodite on Dolphin drawn by wave.

3) Adonis on Boar drawn by Worshipper

4) Leda on Swan drawn by Castor & Pollux

5) Francis of Assisi and his beasts

6) Ariadna on Panther and Dyonisus

7) Andromache on Dragon and Perseus Agnes of Bourganeuf – Pierre d'Aubusson

8) Zizim of Persia

9) Diana on her stag drawn by night.

Pierre D'Aubusson (Duc de la Feuillade) Knight Hospitaller

Zizim of Persia Mohammedan Prince

A fiacre drives up from the left in which *M. Dupetit* and his daughter *Georgette* are seated, homeward bound from a ball.

Georgette is in a very modern and chic gown and wrap.

M. Dupetit is in correct evening dress.   They are waylaid by the revellers, some climb up on the box with the cocher, others hang on to the hood.

Orpheus hands *Georgette* out of the fiacre – her father follows

Orpheus plays – *Georgette* charmed tangos, but gradually the music forces her to rhythmic dancing which becomes bacchanalian (Georgette discards her wrap before she dances, and during her dance the artist removes her modern gown and robe her in some of their glittering things.)

Orpheus and *Georgette* dance. M. Dupetit dances a grotesque dance in which the models join him.

Just as the sun begins to rise Mars appears on a white and gold charger.

Mars dances a greeting to the Sun in which after a time he is joined by all the revellers.

Georgette is helped with her wrap and lifted into the fiacre followed by M. Dupetit.

Farewells –

Flowerladen they depart off right –

– *Mars* leading, Orpheus and his revellers following, they dance off toward the Arc de Triomphe.

The Apache, the waiter and passersby in their wake.

A girl, with a push cart full of Spring blossoms comes along, stops and looks after the revellers shading her eyes with her hand.

TEXTUAL NOTES AND ENDNOTE ANNOTATIONS

I. TEXTUAL NOTES AND ANNOTATIONS FOR CRYSTAL
FLOWERS

THIS VOLUME OF Florine Stettheimer's poetry is based
on the 1949 edition of *Crystal Flowers*, collected and
edited by her sister Ettie Stettheimer (ES), and printed
privately at The Banyan Press in a print run of 250.
The sequence of poems mirrors (with minor variations
within chapters) the ordering of the manuscript versions
contained in the **"Florine and Ettie Stettheimer
Papers," Yale Collection of American Literature,
Beinecke Rare Book and Manuscript Library (YCAL
MSS 20, Series III, Box 8, Folders 133-141)**. A total
of at least 128 poems are extant, of which all except
three, "[All Morning]," "The Masseuse" and "[I Had
been Licking It]," appear in the 1949 edition. We

include these three previously unpublished poems in the Prologue, in the belief that readers should have access to these poems that were excluded either by oversight or error (e.g. "The Masseuse") or because of ES's expressed dislike ("[All Morning]"). Dates in ES's hand on the typescripts suggest that she made final selections in the spring of 1949. The little we know about FS's composition and revision comes from Ettie's foreword to *Crystal Flowers*, which is not reprinted here, but confirms that FS herself had begun the process of collecting some of the poems, as Ettie observes: "Some were slightly emended by her; some collected and arranged in groups, and some few were typed; many I found carelessly left lying about, between the leaves of books or with bills and other business papers." In her notes on the typescripts, for example, ES specifies that some section titles were created by FS including "Nursery Rhymes," "Comestibles," and the "Nature" of the "Nature/ Flora/ Fauna" section. ES also specifies where she created or changed section titles, as she did, for example, for "Americana," and "As Tho' from a Diary," the latter originally titled "Autobiography" by FS. Ettie seemed to vacillate about titling the "People" section "Friends," but opted for the former, and also considered, but then rejected, "Fables" for "Nursery Rhymes." Given the fact that FS herself grouped a number of the poems under clearly defined themes suggests that she considered some sort of publication, but she did not stipulate her intentions clearly, and much suggests that she was conflicted about publicizing her work. It is not clear if FS or Ettie determined the ultimate sequencing of the poems, raising crucial questions that have remained unanswered. For example, was it Ettie or Florine who determined that the sequencing should start with the seemingly simplistic "Nursery" rhymes, instead of with the more complex poetry?

Among the typed poems many exist in two variants, one typed first by FS and another by ES. There are 14 typescripts in the final section, "As Tho' from a Diary" that ES indicates she typed herself from manuscripts and not from FS typescripts. The following poems are extant only in manuscript form: "[A Pink Candy Heart]," "[My Ring Fell from the Nursery Window]," "And Things I Loved – ," "[Schooldays in a Pretty Town]," "First Plastic Art – Herr Gott," "[In Berlin]," "[Art Student Days in New York]," "[In New York]," "[Rome With Streets of Palaces]," "[Paris – Living in the Latin Quarter]," "[Must One Have Models]," "[Munich With Its Carnival]," "[Casein Was Once Milk]," "[Then Back to New York], and "[Primitive Saints]." About 80 of the poems exist in one or more manuscript variants.

A comparison between the 1949 edition of *Crystal Flowers* and the manuscript poems held at Yale provides valuable insight into Ettie's editorial choices. For example, a number of poems appear without titles in the original manuscripts and Ettie proceeded to use the first line as the title by simply setting the line in small capital letters; we follow Ettie's lead but opted for identifying more clearly the use of the first line as title with conventional square brackets. Though ES's handwriting is generally neater and clearer than her sister's, it is not always clear what changes on the typescripts and manuscripts were made by ES or FS herself. However, where Ettie identifies her own edits, they consist primarily of changes in line breaks, punctuation and capitalization for consistency. Almost all of the typescripts contain some variant of Ettie's handwritten approval date "o.k. May 1949." For the most part, where FS includes ellipses in her typescripts, ES removes them. Yet there are some more substantive changes, too, which are identified in the annotations below. In this volume we follow the published 1949 version. In a few rare cases, we make corrections of spelling and punctuation, and in at least one case we insert a word eliminated in Ettie's editing process; all silent corrections are identified and listed in the annotations below.

In the annotations that follow all references to manuscripts and typescripts are from YCAL MSS 20, Series III, Box 8, Folders 133-141; parenthetical page numbers refer to the electronic, on-screen numbering.

[**All Morning**]: 1 MS (Folder 134, 49-50). Written in black ink, this poem was filed in the "Nature Flora Fauna" section but remained unpublished. FS's handwritten note in the bottom margin (50), situates the poem's subject matter and/or composition in "Monmouth Beach August [no year]." Following the poem is a note in pencil, which reveals Ettie's dislike of the poem, "don't like this one ESt," explaining its exclusion from the 1949 edition. An additional handwritten note in Ettie's red pencil, in the top margin preceding the poem's first line, states: "Ought to be re-arrange[d]." Editorial notes include line break revisions and other changes such as, on line 23, replacing "will" with "shall" to establish consistency with "I shall" in lines 24 and 25. In line 17, "It helps – " is amplified in pencil with "It satisfies," and in the poem's original final line, "imitation flowers," "imitation" is crossed out in pencil and replaced with "artificial." garish] garrish

The Masseuse: 1 Typescript (Folder 139, 27-28), with ES's handwritten note in the bottom margin of the first page, "In MSS '49," suggesting that she intended to include this poem in the 1949 edition, but must have either missed it or changed her mind; a blue penciled note confirms that the poem was slated for the "People" section in which it was filed. A penciled note beneath the title reads: "E'S Editing." A red ink notation on the typescript transforms lines 21-22, which originally read, "She gently/ sighed," into one single line, "She gently sighed."

flower embroidered gown] flower embroidered gown..

[**I Had Been Licking It**]: 1 MS (Folder 134, 54). Written in pencil, this poem includes words and edits that are difficult to decipher and attribute. Filed in the "Nature Flora Fauna" section, the unpublished MS begins with what appears to be a false start with the letter "I" set off from the rest of the poem. The word "caressing" in the first line is added above "licking," possibly as an alternative to "licking"; there is also a large and prominent question mark above the two words, querying "licking caressing," or possibly querying inclusion of the entire poem. In the poem's final line, "a bright hued rainbow," a three-letter word that is hard to decipher is tagged on at the end; it looks like "eke," but could also be "etc," or conceivably even "cke," a short form for "cake," to rhyme with "keepsake."

rainbow] rainbow eke

[My Neighbor]: 2 Typescripts (see image on p. 41). ES changes the first line of FS's typescript from "My daughter-in-law" to "My Neighbor," and notes in the margin: "Changed to neighbor by me (E)."

[My Cousin]: 2 Typescripts.

[Mrs. Golden-Pheasant]: 2 Typescripts.

[The Flapper]: 2 Typescripts. In FS's version, the first line "The Cutie" is crossed out by hand and replaced by "The Flapper" in what looks like ES's hand.

[A Llama]: 2 Typescripts.

[Sweet Little Miss Mouse]: 2 Typescripts.

[Miss Cow Called Miss Maisy]: 2 Typescripts. FS's typescript contains a handwritten change in her own hand in which the last two lines are switched.

[Fat Mrs. Pigeon]: 2 Typescripts. FS's typescript contains numerous handwritten additions, changing, for example, "A Pigeon" into "Fat Mrs. Pigeon"; and "With lots of religion" to "Full of religion."

[Mr. Elephant Carried a Spray of Orange Blossom]: 2 Typescripts, one with ES's handwritten note, "I changed division of lines 3 + 4 (ESt)."

[Miss Butterfly]: 2 Typescripts. On FS's typescript, ES crosses out the ellipsis ending the poem and marks "ESt" in the margin. Also line 2, "Was heard to sigh," is crossed-out and replaced with "Sighed a sigh"

[A Foolish Lizzard]: 2 Typescripts.

[Mr. Tango Eel]: 2 Typescripts. On FS's typescript the final line, "but has a permanent wave," is changed to "his permanent wave."

[Miss Lovey Dove]: 2 Typescripts. FS's typescript contains handwritten emendations in the last stanza, changing "We two will fly/ There I will sigh" into "I shall fly/ There I may sigh." Presumably for further clarity, the final stanza with the emendations is recopied by hand at the bottom of the page.

[The Dinosaur]: 2 Typescripts.

[Queer Mr. Bat]: 2 Typescripts.

["Why Should I Care"]: 2 Typescripts.

The Zoo: 2 Typescripts. FS's typescript ends "And it's hard to pair," but the final word is emended by hand to "repair," thus removing the sexual joke of the original line.

[I Like the Air]: 2 Typescripts.

[Young Artist Rat]: 2 Typescripts.

[All She Owned]: 1 Typescript, 1 MS.

NATURE/ FLORA/ FAUNA (FOLDER 134)

Sunrise: 2 Typescripts. FS's types the location and date in the right top margin (West End June 17, 1925). The Stettheimers spent the summer 1925 in West

End, on the New Jersey coast, where their neighbors were the Guggenheims.

[The Sun]: 2 Typescripts. FS's typescript is dated (June 29, 1925).

[This Morning]: 2 Typescripts, 1 MS (see image on p. 53). FS's MS is dated (June 27, West End). Line 9 of ES's typescript contains a change, replacing "form" with "shape."

[Robins Hop]: 2 Typescripts, 1 MS.

The Ocean: 2 Typescripts, 1 MS.

[The Rainbow Shed]: 1 Typescripts, 1 MS.

Spring: 2 Typescripts

[I Planted Greeny-White Petunias]: 1 Typescript, 1 MS.

Breakfast Time: 2 Typescripts. FS's typescript is dated (July 1921). A note appears on ES's indicating her editorial input, "Ed. punctuation changes."

The Revolt of the Violet: 1 Typescripts, 1 MS.

[I Have Hung]: 1 Typescript, 1 MS. In the typescript the title "The Zebra" is crossed out by hand. "I" is inserted in the line "And I whispered," with ES's handwritten note at the bottom confirming, "added the 'I' in line 5th from the end ESt."

[Today]: 1 Typescript, 1 MS.

[Our Privet Hedges Are in Bloom]: 1 Typescript, 1 MS.

The Flutterby: 2 Typescripts.

[Mosquitoes Bite]: 1 Typescript (with two stanzas on two separate pages, as if these were originally two separate poems, and ES's handwritten editorial note in the top left margin, "Combine these 2 into 1," thereby creating a single 2-stanza poem); 1 MS.

Asters: 2 Typescripts, one with ES's handwritten note "Ed. Punctuation/changes to be consistent."

[Our Fancy Pet]: 2 Typescripts.

A Dance: 1 Typescript, 1 MS.

[The Fireflies Are Eaten Up]: 1 Typescript, 1 MS.

Adventure in Larchmont: 2 Typescripts.

The Doves: 1 Typescript dated (June 1925) and situated in West End; 1 MS dated (June 30, 1925).

Ephemère: 1 Typescript; 1 MS titled "An Ephemere," with accents absent in the title and in line 2; ES inserts the accent grave in the typescript version.

THINGS (FOLDER 135)

[My Attitude Is One of Love]: 1 Typescript; 1 MS (19-18); the two final lines are written on a separate page that also contains a diary note recording a failed trip to see the Havemeyer collection of antique Americana belonging to Electra Havemeyer Webb (1888-1960).

The Unloved Painting: 2 Typescripts, 1 MS (see image on p. 67).

My Handkerchief: 2 Typescripts dated (June 20, 1925). A handwritten note on a separate page (17) indicates that the original line "Perfumed Liquid" was replaced by "Perfumed lightness."

Thermos Bottle: 1 Typescript, 1 MS.

[I Found Pink Hearts]: 1 Typescript, 1 MS.

[Mother Asked]: 1 Typescript, 1 MS.

[Art Is Spelled with a Capital A]: 1 Typescript, 1 MS.

COMESTIBLES (FOLDER 136)

[You Beat Me]: 3 Typescripts, 2 MSS.

[You Are Rough]: 2 Typescripts, 1 MS. FS's MS and typescript read, "I am your clay." ES's typescript omits "your," and although she reinserts the word in handwriting, it's missing in the published version. Since it was obviously meant to be in the text, we reinserted it here.

I am your clay] I am clay

[You Stirred Me]: 2 Typescripts, 1 MS (see image on p. 73). The MS reads, "She stirred me/ She made me giddy/ Then she poured…"; in FS's typescript, "she" is replaced in handwriting with "you" in these three lines, providing the final edited version.

[You Called Me a Peach]: 2 Typescripts, 2 MSS.

Stuffed Peppers: 2 Typescripts. The last line on FS's typescript reads: "I breathe more freely again," which is crossed out and replaced with the final version, "I breathe freely once more."

[You Called Me Hog]: 2 Typescripts, 1 MS.

Chaud-Froid: 2 Typescripts.

Tomatoes Russian Dressing: 2 Typescripts.

To P. : 2 Typescripts.

AMERICANA (FOLDER 137)

The note on the section page confirms that the title for this section was chosen by ES: "'Americana'/ my title ESt."

New York: 1 Typescript, 1 MS (see image on p. 81).

Flower Show: 1 Typescript; 1 MS (with ES's handwritten note, "made some changes in spacing ESt").

[Why Call Them]: 1 Typescript, 1 MS.

Prohibition: 1 Typescript (the poem's three versions appear on one page as one unified poem); 1 MS (the three versions appear on three separate pages).

Asbury Park: 1 Typescript with variant closing lines, "Lying stretched/ Along the water/ In the spray," crossed out; 1 MS dated (June 22, no year).

[In the Mus-e-um]: 2 Typescripts.

[The Happy Bride Dropped All]: 1 Typescript, 1 MS.

[Mary, Mary of the]: 1 Typescript, 1 MS.

[This Summer Is Gone]: 1 Typescript, 1 MS.

[I'm Tired]: 1 Typescript, 1 MS.

[Occasionally]: 2 Typescripts.

To a Gentleman Friend: 2 Typescripts, 1 MS.

Narcissus: 2 Typescripts.

A Golden God: 2 Typescripts, 1 MS (see image on p. 87). The line breaks in the original MS are slightly different from those in the typescript and printed version.

Love Poem: 2 Typescripts, one with variant closing lines, "You only obsessed me/ when absent," crossed out; 1 MS which also concludes, "You only obsessed me/ when absent."

[Oh Horrors]: 2 Typescripts, 1 MS.

[You Remind Me]: 2 Typescripts.

[A Golden Youth]: 1 Typescript, 1 MS.

[A Friend Died]: 2 Typescripts. (Bloemink notes that this poem was never printed, but it does appear in the 1949 *Crystal Flowers*, p. 47.)

[You Are Steady Rain]: 1 Typescript, 1 MS

The 13th of October: 2 Typescripts.

[For a Long Time]: 2 Typescripts.

[**Carl**]: 2 Typescripts, one variant of which is located in Folder 140 and dated (July 27, 1924); 1 MS.

[**He Photographs**]: 2 Typescripts, one of which with ES's penciled note in the bottom left corner: "o.k./ May '49/ Shall I ask/ G. what she wants?/ ESt."

C. D. : 1 Typescript, 2 MSS. Ettie's handwritten note on the typescript identifies C.D. as Charles Demuth. The poem refers to painter Charles Demuth's incomplete essay entitled *Three: Georgia O'Keeffe, Florine Stettheimer, Peggy Bacon.* Although he completed only the introduction, the partial essay was published in 1998 by All Kinds Blitzes Press as a fundraiser for the Demuth Foundation. Demuth describes the essay briefly in a letter to Alfred Stieglitz on 12 May 1926; see Charles Demuth and Bruce Kellner, *Letters of Charles Demuth, American Artist, 1883-1935* (Philadelphia: Temple University Press, 2000), 76, n.2.

To Phyllis: 2 Typescripts, with ES's handwritten notes on both, identifying Phyllis as "Phyllis Ackerman."

[**Gertie Met a Unicorn**]: 1 Typescript, with ES's handwritten note identifying Gertie as Gertrude Stein in the bottom left corner; 2 MSS.

P. T.: 1 Typescript; 1 MS, which appears as a letter addressed to "Dear P," beside which the addressee is identified in red pencil as "Pavel Tchelitchew." The epistolary poem runs over two pages with ES's handwritten parenthetical note following the poem's closing lines, ("Don't know whether sent to P. or not)."

Duche: 1 Typescript dated (May 1949) with handwritten alternate title "M.D." crossed out; 1 MS (see image on p. 101).

V. T.: 1 Typescript, 1 MS (untitled and located in folder 138, "Moods," 19). It's likely that ES titled the poem "V.T." Ettie published the last line as "Et Gertrude will protect you all" presuming her sister was playing with the French "And." However, an examination of FS's handwritten manuscript suggests that she more likely intended the word to read "St" as a play on Stein's opera *Four Saints in Three Acts*.

St] Et

[There's Marie Sterner]: 2 Typescripts.

J. S.: 1 Typescript, 1 MS. FS's manuscript, written in blue ink, has the title "J.S." ES's handwritten note on the typescript (dated 1949), "can't place/ J. S. – sounds like Sides/ don't like this p[oem]," suggests that J. S. refers to the art collector and friend of the Stettheimer's Gerald Sides (see Bloemink, *The Life and Art of Florine Stettheimer* 249, n.25), though the initials also match those of painter Joseph Stella (1877-1946). Like FS, Stella had studied at the

Art Student League in New York and his work was exhibited alongside FS's and others in 1924 by the Carnegie Museum International.

[You Did Us Much Harm]: 1 Typescript, 1 MS. The typescript features a title, "Herr Frommer," written in what looks like ES's hand, but the title is subsequently crossed out. FS's manuscript is untitled and written in black pencil with the last four lines crossed out presumably by the same pencil; ES's red editorial pencil marks the end of the poem with an +; beside the crossed out final lines, she writes "omitted" in red pencil, confirming that the following lines are not to be printed: "but we loved the gay silk facings/ of pink, yellow, blue, and green/ they [almost atoned] for the [tortures]/ but unfortunately they could not be seen."

[We Flirted]: 2 Typescripts, 1 MS. On one typescript ES's handwritten note queries punctuation: "Punctuation? Go over orig ms"; on the other she inserts "French" in line 19, "We passed French Liberty," a word that does not appear in FS's manuscript, where "Liberty" is, moreover, given its own separate line.

On a Veranda: 2 Typescripts, one with ES's handwritten note, "Phyllis Ackerman."

[The World is Full of Strangers]: 1 Typescript, 1 MS.

[Look at My]: 1 Typescript, 1 MS.

[They Like a Woman]: 1 Typescript, 1 MS. FS's

manuscript shows that the poem was scribbled in pencil on a small piece of paper (30) and appears to have an additional line written on the verso (31), "The civilizers of the world," which was likely intended by FS either as the poem's title, or as the last line – and omitted in error by ES in the editing.

[Tame Little Kisses]: 1 Typescript, 1 MS.

NOTES TO FRIENDS (FOLDER 140)

[Dear Carlo]: 1 Typescript, 1 MS. The typescript features ES's handwritten approval note: "Probably à propos of 'dedicated to the three of us.'"

[Carlo]: 2 Typescripts, one with ES's handwritten date (o.k. May 1949), and the other with ES's note in black pencil, "incl – Mss/ May '49," followed by a note in red pencil, "under letters T."

To Carl Van Vechten: 3 Typescripts (see image on p. 113). The cleanest variant contains a typed note in the lower right corner of the page, "a propos 'The Tatooed Countess,'" referring to Van Vechten's 1924 novel *The Tattooed Countess*. A second typescript appears on The Copley-Plaza Boston Hotel stationary. The third typescript contains what appears to be a separate but related poem above it: "Florine Stettheimer to Carl Van Vechten (à propos The Tattooed Countess)/ July 27, 1924// Carl/

Carlo/ Carl Van Vechten/ There is Peter/ There is Harold/ There is Gareth/ There'll be others/ Well---/ There is Carl/ Carlo/ Carl van Vechten/ Many thanks/ Florine/ July 27, 1924." There is also a typed note at the bottom, "Originals of above in the New York Public Library," where the Carl Van Vechten Papers are housed.

Houpla Carlo!: 3 Typescripts, one with handwritten date (o.k. May 1919) and note at the bottom, "(à propos 'Firecrackers')," referring to Carl Van Vechten's 1925 novel of the jazz age, *Firecrackers;* there are also some minor corrections in blue pencil.

To Carl: 3 Typescripts, 1 MS (titled "Sweet Moses"). One typescript has the title "To Carl" written in blue ink; on the same page, the final stanza, "Holy Moses/ Lead us to/ Thy Happyland/ We'll follow thee," is crossed out and a note in blue ink, "Use this one," provides the new stanza already typed on the right side of the page (even though this stanza is also crossed out in pencil, this final stanza remained intact in print). There is a note in blue at the bottom confirming the editorial discussion: "Yes, but evidently changed by F[lorine] or sent as note to Carl V. V.? as are some\ the others to C.V.V." Another typescript with a typed dedication confirms that the poem was composed "(à propos Nigger Heaven)," Van Vechten's controversial 1926 novel

Nigger Heaven inspired by Harlem life.

To Dick: 1 Typescript, 1 MS. The typescript has a note in the bottom margin in ES's hand: "o.k./May '49/ Thanks for/ gooseling from/ Richard Schuster," whereas the manuscript note reads: "525 Park Ave/ Richard Shu." The poem itself is an ode to the "cooking" of said gooseling.

[I Tried to Dissect the Marzipan Heart]: 1 Typescript, 1 MS. The typescript is titled "To C" and contains a typed note, "(a propos of Valentine)," followed by a handwritten note, "From Carl V. V. / I think – / not certain." The manuscript contains a handwritten note: "Was this a note of thanks to Carl – / Yes must have been/ see over."

To Philip: 2 Typescripts, one with the dedication "To Phillip Moeller" but "Moeller" is subsequently crossed out with a blue pencil, and the other titled "To P.M." along with a note in red ink, "under letters." FS misspells Philip Moeller's first name with double l, a mistake that is also printed in the 1949 edition.

To Philip] To Phillip

To David P. : 1 Typescript, 1 MS. The manuscript is entitled "To David Proctor" (or Procter), the handwriting of the final letters of the last name being difficult to decipher.

Dear Poet: 1 Typescript, 1 MS.

ES's note on the section title page confirms that "As Tho from a Diary" is ES's title, "My Title-ESt," overriding FS's typed title "Autobiographical."

[A Pink Candy Heart]: 1 Typescript, 1 MS (with ES's note in red pencil, "typed ESt" and note in black pencil, "in MSS/ May 49").

[My Ring Fell from the Nursery Window]: 1 Typescript (line 6 contains an "x" marking a blank space ["to give x   a kiss"] over which "the little rider" in blue ink appears (likely amended by ES). The bottom of the page contains the following note presumably by ES: "x not decipherable/ fill it out with 'the little rider' or singer."

And Things I Loved – : 1 Typescript, 1 MS. A note in red pencil at the bottom of the manuscript page, "Typed and Edited ESt," confirms the editorial changes are ES's. Thus "An adored sash" becomes "Adored sashes." Line 17 of the manuscript, "Mother reading to us Grimms fairy tales," becomes "Mother reading us fairy tales," with ES's encircling "Grimms" and a note explaining, "omitted/ M[other] did not read German ES."

[Schooldays in a Pretty Town]:   1 Typescript, 1 MS. The manuscript begins with 2 lines that appear to be a fragment of another poem; they are demarcated as separate by ES's red pencil and her note: "does not belong here – but where? EST." At the bottom of the page ES writes, "Typed ESt"

First Plastic Art – Herr Gott: 1 Typescript, 1 MS (written in blue ink).

[In Berlin]: 1 Typescript, 1 MS. At the bottom of manuscript ES writes in black pencil, "In Mss May '49" and in red pencil, "Typed Est."

[Art Student Days in New York]: 1 Typescript, 1 MS. At the bottom of the manuscript ES writes in red pencil, "Typed E." In the typescript, ES inserts a line break at line 13, whereby "Emerson and Ruskin Mills and Henry James" becomes "Emerson and Ruskin/ Mills and Henry James."

[In New York]: 1 Typescript, 1 MS. The two-page manuscript reveals the original title, "Diary /Entry – To Art Patron/ New York," which is crossed out; at the bottom of page 2 is ES's note in red pencil, "Typed Est."

[Rome With Streets of Palaces]: 1 Typescript, 1 MS (with ES red-penciled note, "Typed E").

[Paris – Living in the Latin Quarter]: 1 Typescript, 1 MS (with ES red-penciled note, "Typed E"). Written in black ink, the MS contains the original final line "And lunching at Café de la Paix," which is subsequently crossed out in pencil and replaced by the same pencil with "And petit pois à la français –"

[**Must One Have Models**]: 1 Typescript (in line 5, ES's blue pen capitalizes "The Blue Hat"); 1 MS (with ES red-penciled note, "Typed E").

[**Munich With Its Carnival**]: 2 Typescripts, 1 MS (with ES red-penciled note, "Typed").

[**Casein Was Once Milk**]: 2 Typescripts (one with alternate title "Munich"); 1 MS (with alternate title "My Diary – Munich" and with ES's red-penciled note "Typed E").

[**Then Back to New York**]: 2 Typescripts (one typescript shows the poem titled "7./ Then Back to New York" followed on the same page by the poem titled "8./ New York," as if they were meant to be together, but the second poem is subsequently crossed out); 1 MS (with ES red-penciled note, "Typed").

[**Primitive Saints**]: 1 Typescript, 1 MS (2 pages with title "Diary New York" and with ES red-penciled note at the bottom of the second page, "Typed E").

New York: 2 Typescripts (one appearing beneath "Then Back to New York," but crossed out).

[**Which –**]: 1 Typescript, 1 MS. In the manuscript, in line 14, ES identifies a deletion by marking "and gab fests" in red and adding the note "omitted E."

[**Our Parties**]: 1 Typescript, 1 MS dated "about 1917" and titled "Diary New York" (see image on p. 121). In the MS, FS (or ES?) changes line 7 from "They amuse me enough" to "It amuses me"; and line 8 from "To turn them into pictures" to "To recreate them."

2. TEXTUAL NOTE ON ORPHÉE OF THE QUAT-Z-ARTS

THERE ARE THREE close variants of Stettheimer's previously unpublished libretto for her ballet "Orphée of the Quat-z-arts or The 4 Arts Revellers" first drafted in 1912. Over the years, FS would continue to sketch, paint, and make models of costumes and set designs for the ballet. Two fairly complete variants interspersed with fragments, notes, and sketches are contained in the Florine and Ettie Stettheimer Papers at Yale (YCAL MSS 20 Series III folder 142). The first of the Yale variants (hereafter referred to as "Yale 1"), is subtitled "A Choreographic Drama" and contains four distinct scene notations, as well as speaking lines that announce and explicate each character's role, followed by a brief and fragmentary appendix. The second Yale variant (hereafter referred to as "Yale 2") contains no speaking lines and is devoid of scenic notation. The third variant is contained at the Museum of Modern Art Special Collections Library in New York and, although ambiguously dated as "[1916?]" in the library catalogue, according to the notes prefacing both Yale and MoMA variants, it does indeed appear to be the most authoritative variant. The MoMA variant is the cleanest with the least number of changes and crossed-out sections, lending the document an aura of finality consistent with its metadata, and as such, is our chosen copytext.

The two Yale variants with fragments and sketches, begin with a note (written presumably in the hand of Ettie Stettheimer) which reads: "Florine Stettheimer's / earlier libretti etc./ for her ballet/ 'Quarts' Art'/ Original sketches + / Models in / Museum of Modern/ Art/ New York." On the following page appears a large Roman numeral I in red ink in the top right hand corner, as well as a note in black ink identifying it as: "Florine's Ballet/ (earlier libretto/ with words)." Accordingly, a Roman numeral II appears on the cover page of the MoMA variant followed by a note in the same hand as the notes preceding the Yale variants identifying the manuscript as "Florine's Ballet/ (Later Libretto/ without words)." Nonetheless, the MoMA variant is extremely close to Yale 2.

The MoMA houses 43 elaborate costume and scenery designs for the ballet in the form of drawings, paintings, and puppets prepared by FS. Many of these use an array of materials including oil, beads, and metal lace on canvas.

110: candles] candle

110: quietly] word preceding "quietly" is illegible. Possibly reads "quietly, quietly" in error.

113: with her hand.] with her hand

ABBREVIATIONS AND ALLUSIONS

Adonis: In Greek myth, a handsome youth killed by a boar.

Alwyn Court: Located at 58th and Seventh Avenue, the site for the Stettheimer sisters' salon from 1926 on. Today a New York City landmark.

Les Ambassadeurs: Luxury restaurant decorated in Rococo style located at the foot of Les Champs Elysées, at the north end of the Place de la Concorde.

André Brook: River that separates Tarrytown and Sleepy Hollow, New York, where the Stettheimer sisters had their summer residence; here on July 28, 1917, Marcel Duchamp celebrated his 30th birthday. André Brook is featured in FS's poetry and painting.

Andromache: In Homer's *Iliad*, Andromache is the wife of Hector, the outstanding Trojan warrior; she is taken captive after the Trojans lose the war.

Aphrodite: Born of the sea foam, Aphrodite is the Greek goddess of love, beauty, and sexuality.

Ariadna: *Ariadne on the Panther* (1810-1824) is a famous sculpture by German artist Johann Heinrich von Dannecker. The mythological Ariadne is married to Dionysus.

Asbury Park: On the New Jersey coast, known for its beaches and musical tradition. FS refers to it in her poetry and captures its carnival, mixed-race beach party atmosphere in her painting *Asbury Park South* (1920).

Bedford Hills: A hamlet in northern Westchester County, New York, referred to in FS's poetry and painting. *Picnic at Bedford Hills* (1918) is held at the Pennsylvania Academy of Fine Arts.

C.D.: Charles Demuth (1883-1935), American water-color painter and member of the Stettheimer salon.

Campaspe: The mistress of Alexander the Great and model for Apelles' painting of Venus rising out of the sea.

Carl or **Carlo:** Carl Van Vechten (1880-1964), bisexual photographer, writer, and critic; close friend of the Stettheimers and frequent presence at their salon.

Casein: FS used Casein, or milk paint, a technique she learned in Munich. See Herr Apotheker F.

Castor & Pollux: In Greek and Roman mythology, twin off-spring of Leda and Zeus/Tyndareus, associated with the constellation Gemini.

Les Champs Elysées: Luxury avenue running from Place de la Concorde to the Arc de Triomphe in Paris.

Charles Henri Ford: (1908-2002), surrealist poet and co-author (with Parker Tyler) of *The Young and the Evil* (1933), an experimental novel with openly homosexual subject matter. Ford's longtime partner Parker Tyler is FS's first biographer, *Florine Stettheimer: A Life in Art* (1963).

David P: David Proctor or Procter, presumably a Stettheimer friend.

Diana on her stag: Roman goddess of the hunt and the woodlands.

Dick: ES identifies him as Richard Schuster, presumably a Stettheimer friend.

Duche: Marcel Duchamp (1887-1968), close friend of the Stettheimer sisters, especially Ettie. FS's nickname for the artist is a pun on French *duc* (duke) and *douche* (shower) and it is also one of Duchamp's many pseudonyms.

Edna: Edna Kenton (1876-1954), sister of Mabel Reber, fiction writer, feminist, executive committee member of the Provincetown Players, and close friend of Carl Van Vechten until a falling out in 1934.

ES or **ESt:** Ettie Stettheimer (1875-1955), philosopher and writer; Florine's sister and literary executor.

Euridice: The Greek mythological nymph Eurydice dies when she steps on a snake; her distraught husband Orpheus descends into the underworld to retrieve her.

Fania: Fania Marinoff (1890-1971), the Russian-American actress, was Carl Van Vechten's second wife and a regular presence at the Stettheimer salon.

Francis of Assisi: (1181-1226), Italian Catholic patron saint of animals.

FS: Florine Stettheimer (1871-1944), poet, painter, set designer.

Georgia: Georgia O'Keeffe (1887-1986), American painter and friend of FS; she delivered a eulogy when FS died.

Gertie: Gertrude Stein (1874-1946), American avant-garde poet and author of the libretto *Four Saints and Three Acts*, whose production involved set design by FS and music by Virgil Thomson.

Herr Apotheker F.: (Mr. Pharmacist F.) A Munich art instructor under whom Stettheimer took lessons while traveling with her family between 1900-1914.

Herr Frommer: Unidentified.

J.S.: ES conjectures that he may be Stettheimer friend Gerald Sides, and Bloemink suggests he may be art collector James Loeb (1867-1933), but the initials also point to painter Joseph Stella. His identity cannot be determined conclusively.

Knights Hospitaller: Christian order founded in the 11th century in the Holy Land to help the poor.

Lake Placid: Village and lake in the Adirondack Mountains, and subject of FS's poetry and painting including *Lake Placid* (1919) held in the Museum of Fine Arts in Boston.

Larchmont: Village in Westchester County, New York and summer resort frequented by the Stettheimers.

Leda: In Greek mythology, Leda was raped by Zeus who disguised himself as a swan.

Mabel: Mabel Reber, née Kenton, Edna Kenton's sister, a society reporter and occasional costume designer for the Provincetown Players, who boarded cats in her Greenwich Village apartment where Carl Van Vechten visited regularly.

Maggie: Margaret Burguess, Florine Stettheimer's Irish governess.

Marcel: Marcel Duchamp. See Duche.

Marie: Marie Sterner (1877-1953), wife of New York illustrator and painter Albert Sterner (1863-1946). Steiner was on staff at the Knoedler Gallery in New York and in 1920, opened her own gallery for contemporary art at 556 Fifth Avenue.

Mars: In Roman mythology, Mars is the god of war.

Orpheus: In Greek mythology Orpheus is a musician and poet said to charm people with his lyre; he descends into the underworld to retrieve his wife Euridice.

P.T.: Pavel Tchelitchew (1898-1957), surrealist painter whose work FS viewed at the Museum of Modern Art, and who also visited her salon. Tchelitchew was the partner of Charles Henri Ford, also referred to in FS's poetry.

Peggy: Peggy Bacon (1895-1987), an American writer, illustrator, and artist well known for her satirical portrait caricatures.

Peter: Carl Van Vechten's fictional alter ego Peter Whiffle appearing in his autobiographical novel *Peter Whiffle, His Life and Work* (1922).

Philip: Philip Moeller (1880-1958), New York director and producer. He was a co-founder of the Washington Square Players and frequent visitor at the Stettheimer salon.

Phyllis: Phyllis Ackerman (1893-1977), Persian Art Historian. With her husband, Arthur Upham Pope, Ackerman founded the American Institute for Persian Art and Archeology.

Pierre d'Aubusson: Duc de la Feuillade (1423-1503), cardinal involved in the crusade against the Turks;

elected grand master of the Hospital in 1476. See Knights Hospitaller.

Quat-z-arts ball: Ball of the Four Arts (architecture, painting, sculpture, and engraving), masked ball and all-night pagan revel organized annually in the spring by the students of the École des Beaux Arts in Paris.

Sophie: The title of Philip Moeller's 1919 comedy, depicting a night in the life of French actress Sophie Arnould (1740-1802). Published by Knopf with a foreword by Carl Van Vechten, the book was adorned with yellow paper boards alluded to in FS's poem.

St.: Florine Stettheimer. See FS.

Stokowski: Leopold Stokowski (1882-1977), American conductor.

V.T.: Virgil Thomson (1896-1989), American composer with whom FS collaborated on the opera for Gertrude Stein's libretto *Four Saints in Three Acts.*

Zizim of Persia: (1459-1495), Ottoman prince and poet exiled in France in the fabled Zizim Tower in the town of Bourganeuf from 1486 to 1488.

CHRONOLOGY

1871, AUGUST 19: Florine Stettheimer is born in Rochester, New York, to a wealthy family of German-Jewish immigrants, Joseph Stettheimer, a banker, and Rosetta Walter. Her elder siblings are Stella, Caroline "Carrie," and Walter.

1875, JULY 31: Henrietta "Ettie" Stettheimer, Florine's youngest sister, is born.

1870s: The Stettheimer family travel to Europe. When Joseph deserts the family during FS's childhood, the family stays in Europe (mainly Stuttgart and Berlin) until the early 1890s. Their governess is Margaret "Maggie" Burgess, an Irish Catholic, and FS's art teacher in Stuttgart is Fräulein Sophie von Prieser.

1890s: Return to New York.

1892, OCTOBER: FS enrolls in the Art Students League at 215 West 57th Street in New York, studying with Carroll Beckwith, Kenyon Cox, and Henri Roberts, while Ettie pursues academic studies at Columbia

University, graduating with an MA in psychology in 1898.

1898: The Stettheimer family spend time traveling in Europe until 1914. In 1903, Ettie earns her PhD in philosophy at the University of Freiburg with a dissertation on William James.

1910: FS rents a studio in Munich until 1913. FS hand-paints Bavarian china plates, and attaches a typewritten poem in German on the verso of the plate: "And, as far as art is concerned, I am not / worried about comparison with the great" (Francis M. Naumann Fine Art, New York).

1912, AUGUST: Gertrude Stein's word-portraits of Matisse and Picasso appear in Alfred Stieglitz's *Camera Work*.

1912: FS first conceives of her ballet "Orphée of the Quat-z-arts or The Revellers of the 4 Arts Ball," but will rework this draft numerous times and continue to create paintings and models of costume and set designs. In 1916 FS discusses the possibility of producing "Orphée" with Ballet Russes member Adolph Bolm, but the production never materializes.

1914: Permanent return to New York. FS establishes a residence with her mother and two sisters Carrie and Ettie in her aunt's Manhattan townhouse at 102 West 76th Street. FS spends most of the day working in her studio in the Beaux Arts Building on West 40th Street and decorates both the family home and her studio in her distinctive style. She paints and writes poetry.

1915: FS and her sisters Carrie and Ettie begin to host salons that will continue for three decades. When FS finishes a painting, she invites 20-25 artist friends for dinner for the unveiling. FS's friends include, among many others, Henry McBride, Carl Van Vechten, Marcel Duchamp, and Georgia O'Keeffe.

1916: FS visits Lake Placid in the Adirondacks with her family.

1916, OCTOBER: Solo exhibition of FS's work in Knoedler Gallery in New York curated by Marie Sterner (who would open the Marie Sterner Gallery in New York in 1920).

1917: Ettie publishes *Philosophy: An Autobiographical Fragment*, about her time as a doctoral student at Freiburg University; she uses the pseudonym Henrie Waste.

1923: Ettie publishes her autobiographical novel *Love Days*. FS begins to sign her name as Florine "St."

1926: FS and her family move to Alwyn Court at 182 West 58th Street.

1934: FS designs the sets and costumes for Virgil Thomson and Gertrude Stein's opera *Four Saints in Three Acts*.

1935: FS's mother dies and FS, for the first time, sets up her separate residence independent of her sisters in her studio apartment on West 40th Street.

1937, JULY: FS visits Canada with Ettie and Carrie.

1944, MAY 11: FS dies after a two-year battle with cancer; Carrie dies suddenly 6 weeks later. Ettie becomes the sole executor of FS and Carrie's work.

1946: Florine Stettheimer Retrospective at the Museum of Modern Art, New York.

1949: Ettie edits, introduces, and publishes privately FS's poems in *Crystal Flowers*.

1955, JUNE 1: Ettie dies. Joseph Solomon becomes executor of FS's work.

ACKNOWLEDGEMENTS

THE POETRY OF FLORINE STETTHEIMER was a true discovery and a pleasure to present. We wish to thank the graduate students in Communication and Culture at Ryerson University who have taught us about Florine Stettheimer and her work through their engagement of the poetry, most notably Rachel Frohlich. We would like to thank the Modern Literature and Culture Research Center at Ryerson University, dedicated to the study and preservation of modernist women's texts, for providing a fertile environment for this type of collaborative research and recovery of texts; Joanna Cafua, Saeed Teebi, Erin McCurdy, Juan Ilerbaig, and Karen McEwen.

We thank the staff at Yale University, Beinecke Rare Book and Manuscript Library, where Florine Stettheimer's poetry is held. In our extensive copyright searches we have been grateful for the information provided by numerous persons: Nancy Kuhl, Curator of Poetry, Yale Collection of American Literature; Jennifer B. Lee, Columbia University; Francis M. Naumann, New York; Michael Ryan, Columbia University; Jane Siegel, Columbia University; Jerome Solomon and assistant Angie Fitzpatrick, New York; Jenny Tobias, Museum of Modern Art. While every effort has been made to locate copyright holders, the editors would be happy to hear of any errors or oversights.

We are grateful to the scholarly sleuthing that has preceded ours, most notably to Barbara J. Bloemink, whose biography *The Life and Art of Florine Stettheimer* has been an invaluable resource; as well as scholarship provided in the work of Emily Bilski, Emily Braun, Donna Graves, Linda Nochlin, David Tatham, Parker Tyler, and Steven Watson. We hope this volume builds on their work in new and important ways.

We thank the editors at BookThug for enthusiastically taking on this project, and in particular, Jay MillAr for his artistic vision for this book.

The preparation of this book would not have been possible without the generous support of the Canada Research Chairs program, the Canada Foundation for Innovation, and the Social Sciences and Humanities Research Council of Canada. We also thank Ryerson University, the Vice-President for Research and Innovation, the Dean of Arts, and the English Department for support granted through the university's Postdoctoral Fellowship program.

Modern Literature and Culture Research Center
Ryerson University, Toronto
www.ryerson.ca/mlc

ABOUT THE EDITORS

IRENE GAMMEL holds the Canada Research Chair in Modern Literature and Culture at Ryerson University in Toronto. She is the author of numerous books including *Baroness Elsa*, a biography of New York Dada artist and poet Elsa von Freytag-Loringhoven, and *Looking for Anne*, revealing the hidden life of Canadian author L.M. Montgomery during the writing of her classic novel *Anne of Green Gables.*

SUZANNE ZELAZO is a poet and postdoctoral fellow at the Modern Literature and Culture Research Center, Ryerson University, where she researches avant-garde women's poetics and performance. She is the author of *Parlance*, a volume of poetry channeling, among others, Leonard Cohen and Virginia Woolf.

COLOPHON

Manufactured in an edition of 500
copies by BookThug in the Fall
of 2010. Second printing, 2015.
Distributed in Canada by the Literary
Press Group: www.lpg.ca. Distributed
in the US by Small Press Distribution:
www.spdbooks.org. Shop on-line at
www.bookthug.ca

BOOK
PRODUCTION
WAR ECONOMY
STANDARD

Type + design by Jay MillAr